EDISON 64

*For
Terry A. Williamson and
the Philadelphia Vietnam Veterans
Fund Board of Directors*

EDISON 64
A Tragedy in Vietnam and at Home

By

Award Winning Author and Historian
Richard Sand

For Our Veterans of the Vietnam War
and their Families

Copyright © 2018 by Richard Sand, All rights reserved.

No part of this book may be reproduced in any form or by any electronic or mechanical means, including information storage and retrieval systems, without permission in writing from the publisher, except by reviewers, who may quote brief passages in a review.

Printed in the United States Of America

First Printing March 2018

For information: Righter's Mill Press
475 Wall Street
Princeton, NJ 08540

Library of Congress Cataloging-in-Publication Data
Sand, Richard 5-1-1943
EDISON 64/ Richard Sand
ISBN: 978-1-948460-00-2

First Edition

Jacket Designed by Brian Hailes

All photographs credited by individuals under captions of the photo

Visit our Web Site at:
http://www.rightersmill.com

Other Books by Richard Sand

Fiction

Tunnel Runner

Private Justice

Hands of Vengeance

Watchman with a Hundred Eyes

Hell's Reunion

Blood Redeemed

The Immortal Doctor Fu Manchu

Coming Soon

Death Wave

Terrorists in Wonderland

Non-Fiction

Protocol - The Complete Handbook of Official, Diplomatic, and Social Usage (25th Anniversary Edition)

Protocol - The Complete Handbook of Official, Diplomatic, and Social Usage (30th Anniversary Edition)

Girard College - A Living History

"We love you, young men of Edison."—

Robert Wayne Clarke, Principal of Edison High School, announced daily on the school public address system.

In Appreciation

My deepest appreciation to the Edison 64 who sacrificed their lives for our Country and to those Edison servicemen and their families who opened their hearts and homes to me, and

To Dr. Darryrl Johnson, USAF Retired, and Edison 64 Historian,

To Al Longden, my literary agent and member of the Special Forces for four years in the Vietnam War; and,

The Vietnam Veterans Memorial Fund; and,

The Philadelphia Vietnam Veterans Memorial Fund

Table of Contents

Preface xi
Overview xv
Prologue xvii

Chapter 1 – The Castle 1
Chapter 2 – Faculty Interviews 5
Chapter 3 – The War 19
Chapter 4 – The War at Home 25
Chapter 5 – They Served and Survived 31
Chapter 6 – Lost but not Forgotten—The Edison 64 109
Chapter 7 – Remembrances of Those who Gave their Lives . . 175
Chapter 8 – The Deepest Wounds 197
Chapter 9 – The VA 207
Chapter 10 – Memorials 213

Epilogue 223
Author's Note 225
About the Author 227

x

Preface

In December 1965, I joined the United States Army. Fresh out of high school, in love with my high school sweetheart, and in receipt of a draft notice, I thought volunteering would be the better part of valor, or some would say, the worst part of stupidity. It was neither. Rather it was the beginning of who I am.... the beginning of me. It has been a long and circuitous route to the man I am today.

Within my first five months of service, my mother got an unannounced and exceedingly frightening visit by two FBI agents. After she nearly fainted, they divulged they were simply checking the validity of my character to confirm a requested security clearance. Shortly after, with clearance in hand, I was assigned to the 1st Special Forces Group in Okinawa, wherein 1966, our mission was primarily secret operations in the Pacific region to include support operations and training operations in South East Asia.

Our unit had the sad distinction of having the first casualty of the Vietnam War, (Captain Harry Cramer killed 21 October 1957).

After thirteen months in Okinawa, I was reassigned to the 82nd Airborne Division, Ft. Bragg, North Carolina, where I barely unpacked my bags before I was off again to Vietnam. I entered "Nam" on a military charter jet. The harrowing emergency landing resulted in three flat tires, my brothers-in-arms and I racing across an exploding tarmac and our diving behind sandbags due to a rare mortar attack at Tan Son Nhut Air Base. Welcome to Vietnam indeed! I spent three weeks there getting my orders, preparing for my assignment, and gathering the necessary data I would need for my ultimate destination, Thailand. I would visit Vietnam four other times during the next two-plus years.

It was a surreal place for an outsider, this Vietnam. Three of my visits were in and around Saigon, the fourth in Nha Trang. You could often hear the sound of bombs and sometimes even feel the concussion under your feet. Small arms and automatic weapons fire were common in the suburbs and terrorist-style attacks on bars and nightclubs were watched for with uncommon vigilance. All this danger, suspicion and chaos were subverted by the ever-present sound of music emanating from the bars and clubs.

The laughter and dancing and alcohol and pot and Thai sticks and opium and the unbelievably beautiful, sleek, petite, and accommodating bar girls, gave you the very wrong impression that no one was dying. That no one had lost an arm, a leg, or half a face. It was unimaginable for a visitor like me to believe a war was raging around us. Not until it was time for one of your comrades to return to their unit in the field. The field where one lived with constant tension, not fear per se, but tension, never-ending, forcing you to be always alert, always aware that the kid you just helped could be the next Viet Cong to shoot at you.

It was a place of uncommon heroes and unscrupulous bastards, but mostly just guys and forgotten servicewomen, trying to survive another day in the heat and humidity among a strange and beautiful people they were there to help.

Vietnam.... Every death, every life-changing injury suffered, took a piece out of all of us that served during those hellacious years. Those pieces that cost us all a measure of sadness and guilt for not being able to do something, anything, to bring all those lives back to us, whole and alive and productive. To explain why a nation deserted us.

I have been Literary Agent for Mr. Richard Sand for nearly ten years. Over this time, he has become my friend and colleague. What he has so artfully written and dramatically put together about this unfortunately unique high school in North Philadelphia, cannot answer all the myriad of questions that many of those who served still carry, but it goes some distance with its empathy to assuage those feelings that continue to haunt us. For that, I am most grateful.

Albert T. Longden
Former Staff Sargent, 46th Special Forces Company (ABN),
1st Special Forces Group, Lop Burl Thailand

Overview

"Edison High School," now known as Thomas Alva Edison High School and John C. Fariera Skills Center, is a co-ed, multi-racial secondary school located in North Philadelphia. It initially opened in 1907 as an all-male institution, featuring vocational instruction in the 11th and 12th grades. Edison is in "North Philly," a part of the City, which like much of the rest, is composed of neighborhoods where each 4–6 block area was its own village, complete with its prized corners and the local grocery store. Folks looked after each other and trespassers had explaining to do.

At the high school, the neighborhoods came together, with two stone lions as guardians and its school colors of yellow and green. Edison even had its own "battle cry" they called it, so when the young men faced their rivals or the gangs, they did so as brothers. "Edison Mambo" they would chant, "Edison Mambo, Olé Olé!"

In the late 60s and 70s, jobs were hard to come by, so many of the students selected the Armed Forces instead of waiting for the rare opportunity of welding, commercial art, or auto mechanics, or even the more common and poorly paying jobs running errands or the like. This resulted in a momentous and sickening piece of history.

The school became the home of 64 lives lost in the Vietnam War, more than at any other school in the nation. Many other fine young men, black, white, Hispanic, survived only to have their lives tortured by the effects of combat wounds, cancer and other diseases caused by Agent Orange, and harrowing Post-Traumatic Stress Disorder.

Thanks to the tireless assistance of Air Force Veteran, Dr. Darryrl Johnson, recently retired from Edison, and the courage and trust of those who spoke to me, I have had the opportunity and honor of interviewing dozens of former soldiers as well as family members who have survived their fallen. Each time, I have found myself reeling from the recollection of those lives that were ended or broken. I have supplemented these interviews with research about the times, the neighborhoods, and the War.

Edison High maintained a fraternal tradition that incoming freshmen were to kiss the backside of the stone lions in front of the school. Most students did. But nobody at all expected that the future, like jungle beasts, would tear the school's young men to pieces, leaving only their stories, which I dare to tell, and their brotherhood which I am not worthy to share.

Prologue

It was an experience that I had almost sixty years ago, that started me on the path to this important project. It was nothing that happened to hurt or scar me with trauma, but what occurred was unforgettable and clearly, the beginning, even if compared to the War, it was in such an almost silly circumstance.

I was a member of my family's bowling team, except for Lou Brosman, who smoked a pipe and could have passed for anyone's uncle, but in fact was no relative of mine at all. There we were, "The Sandbros," Sand, Sand, Sand, Sand, and Brosman in our matching shirts, attacking the pins in the hanger-like Bowlero at 69th and Marshal Roads in Upper Darby, Pennsylvania.

We were there on Tuesday nights for pretty much of June through August. Only rich folks, which we certainly were not, went away for the summer "down the shore." We got to play this game as if the competition mattered. There I saw him, this large balding man, sitting on one of those pastel plastic chairs. He was hiding his face in his big hands and crying so much that his body was shaking.

"What's wrong with him?" I asked my uncle Percy.

"It just happens to him sometimes," I was told. "He was in the war."

"Is there something…." I tried.

"Let him be," my older brother told me. My brother was in the Army himself and home on leave.

I remember that man crying as if it were yesterday. Somehow, he's been crying and shaking from when I was a teenager until now. And I still sometimes wonder why he didn't get up and leave or why somebody didn't do something for him.

My brother, Steve, went back to serve his country a couple of days later. He wears hearing aids in both ears from a grenade explosion. I never saw the crying man again, and I don't know his name, but I'll never forget him.

It was about a dozen years or one war later, and I was doing these entertainment shows, an odd combination of daredevil martial arts, breaking boards that were on fire, fighting two or three guys who were armed with knives and with that, telling jokes, which weren't half bad. I had done a couple of hundred shows at the time, so I guess it was all pretty enjoyable.

I had an agent of sorts and the speaker's bureau got me appearances. One of them happened to be at The Valley Forge Military Hospital where I would be again some years later, but for a much different reason.

I figured the audience would enjoy all the action and things would go well. I couldn't have been more wrong. So, I do my magician and clown act, which usually gets the audience into it. The fighting stuff, I'm thinking's going to generate some interest or enthusiasm. But nothing happened. You could hear a pin drop. Every face was completely blank. It was like I was looking at a row of empty windows, which made me feel like I did when I saw that crying man.

I had to do something with those feelings I was carrying around with me. So, when I finally got myself into serious writing, I knew what I had to do. My first published book was about what war does to its heroes. *Tunnel Runner* received terrific reviews about the main character, Ashman, in a "turning action nightmare." *Today's Librarian* wrote, "Fans of the espionage thriller rejoice!" and *Rap-*

Prologue   xix

port Magazine gave the recounting of the hero facing his Vietnam horror, a star review.

In *Tunnel Runner*, we see Ashman as he felt himself running in the slippery mud as turning stars went on and on like a fiery wheel. He ran faster and faster, looking for a place where he could cross over the blood-red mud that appeared more and more as he ran. And all the ones that he had lost and ones that he had killed and the ones he kept locked away in his memory, ran on with him, and he ran with these metal men, in and out of them, like they were standing still, their faces up and down and bleeding.

A tiny part of the suffering and craziness of what happened in Vietnam was inside of me now, although certainly not as it is for those who were "in country." I am not sure why, perhaps because of my own crazy life, or perhaps, just because I am human. Sometimes, I think I was meant to help tell the stories of those who were there, so all would know of The Edison 64 and what it means. I once read a novel by Orson Scott entitled, *Speaker for the Dead*. Maybe it's like that.

Then years passed, and I wrote a number of other well-reviewed books, both fiction and non-fiction. One of the latter was about the history of Girard College, which I think had something to do with my getting appointed to The Pennsylvania Historical and Museum Commission on which I served under Governors Tom Corbett and Tom Wolf.

In that capacity, I often volunteered to represent the Commission in the unveiling of historic markers. One of them turned out to be at The Valley Forge Military Hospital, which I had been so affected by years before. I was standing there about to ceremoniously unveil the ten-foot marker with a World War II veteran in his service uniform.

"I don't feel worthy to be here," I said.

"Me, either," he told me, to my surprise.

"Excuse me," I said. "I don't understand."

"I came home," he said.

We both had tears in our eyes.

Some months later, I was dedicating a marker for the Edison 64. I read the copy of the monument and their application. The story of those 64 students who had died left me numb, and I sat in my car a long time before I could carry out my assignment of dedicating the monument.

In any case, I went and did my job in the parking lot of this shopping center where an earlier edition of Edison had once stood. Politicians were having their say and members of the VFW and so on. I met Dr. Darryrl Johnson, who was overseeing things and later made this book possible. There were vets in various Vietnam t-shirts, speeches, photos of the dead and the playing of taps, and then I left. I didn't belong there with the hand-shaking and embraces. I had no brotherhood to share.

So, I walked around the corner to my car. I wept when I got home and called Dr. Johnson to see if I could meet some of those who served, to learn and tell their stories.

I remember the first two more than the others. Though I had interviewed hundreds of people for other projects and written a dozen books, somehow, I was nervous as I went out to meet George Bembischew and then, Donna Swift Plummer. I made wrong turns and then had to call to get directions.

Yet when we sat down to talk, all went well, dramatic, and heart-rending, but with pride and resolve, I hope that comes through and their voices stay with you.

CHAPTER ONE

The Castle

In 1988, The School District of Philadelphia opened the new Edison High School as the Thomas Alva Edison High School and John C. Fariera Skills Center at 151 West Luzerne Street in North Philadelphia. Housed in a structure of modern brick design, complete with its own athletic field, significant greenery, and spacious auditorium, it offers both vocational training and academic and college preparatory education. The student body, which is largely Latino and African American is composed of more than 1,300 boys and girls in grades 9–12, served by approximately 150 teachers. What perpetuated this institution and community from the early 1900s is a fascinating and often difficult history.

The initial undertaking at the beginning of the twentieth century was a gothic structure at Eighth Street and Lehigh Avenue, designed by architect, Lloyd Titus, to appear like a castle from the Middle Ages, complete with turrets, gargoyles, and those stone lions at the entrance. As Warren Loeb of *The Philadelphia Inquirer* wrote in 1982, it was "seemingly built to fend off the attack." Unfortunately, this was an objective that it could not achieve for long.

When first opened, with its grand auditorium, the then Northeast Manual Training School was considered a prestigious institution for the training of industrial workers for the many mills and factories in the neighborhood, the most notable being the Quaker Lace factory, just four blocks away. Such dignitaries as Albert Einstein, Babe Ruth, and Amelia Earhart came to visit and observe. Comfortable housing was put up for the largely white workers, who made good wages and sent their children to the school to learn similarly productive trades.

But things began to change and not for the better, with what is dispassionately referred to as the "deindustrialization" of the area. In 1912, the school was renamed, "Northeast High School." The factories closed and as they did, their workers moved away.

By the 1950s, Northeast High School relocated to Cottman and Algon Avenues in what some say was clearly an act of racism. Even the school's athletic trophies were taken to the white neighborhood. What was left behind was a school for the poor and minorities. In an attempt to reinvigorate the spirit of industry, the remaining structure was renamed after the inventor, Thomas Alva Edison, who ironically only attended school himself for a few months.

The once imposing factories were now cavernous shells surrounding Edison High School and the comfort of financial stability was gone. Yet the school and the community remained, held together by the warmth of the families and their commitment to the neighborhood.

The Uptown Theater for instance, once had seating for more than 2,000 and high ceilings and stained-glass windows for the pleasure of the long-gone executives whose mansions once lined the streets in the days of industrial wealth. Then later, the theater ran rock 'n roll shows hosted by Georgie Woods of radio station WDAS and Jocko Henderson of WHAT. Sam Reed led the house band for the performances of such stars as Flip Wilson, James Brown, The Supremes and Ike and Tina. Soon that changed, too.

Terrible destruction came in the 1960s. War abroad and war at home, the Vietnam War, and the infamous Philadelphia gang wars, which brought death to the neighborhood at the hands of local criminal organizations, such as The Valley, The Zulu Nation, 20th and Diamond, 15th and Oxford, and the OK Corral. Each gang was composed of peewees, midgets, juniors, seniors, and old heads and could have as many as 500 members. This meant rampant dope-dealing, robberies, and murders, so many that the gang deaths were published in the papers alongside those from the Vietnam War. The scourge of gangland violence continued without abatement until the pledge of "Imani" initialed by the House of Umoja (Unity) on January 1, 1974.

At the same time, employment, even part-time jobs, became harder and harder for students and graduates of Edison to secure, as unemployment was at 20% and the annual income only slightly more than $3,000. So, as one Edison student said, "I'd rather get shot while in uniform and earning a paycheck than left dead in my street by some gangbanger who capped me for the fun of it." Thus, almost 70% of those from North Philly who went off to fight in Vietnam, had volunteered.

On August 28, 1964, it was as if all the street violence came together in the Columbia Avenue riots. There were three nights of looting, fires, property destruction and attacks in North Philadelphia. This resulted in millions of dollars of damage and injuries to 300 civilians and one hundred police officers.

Edison High student, Curtis Thomas, who was already working odd jobs to support his family, was quoted by Will Bunch of the *Daily News*: "All of the anger and hopelessness was just let out."

The destruction continued as Edison began to crumble figuratively and literally. A total of 648 men from Philadelphia died in Southeast Asia. Sixty-four of them were students from Edison High School, the largest number of any high school in the Nation. With that and the gang killings, the students were becoming immune to horror. When Principal Glassman would announce over the PA system that another classmate had died in Southeast Asia, his audience was not shocked or horrified, for their friends and neighbors had just as likely been killed just around the corner.

Eventually, The Castle was gutted and set on fire. A strip mall replaced its ruins. The students and the school were relocated to Front and Luzerne, the present location.

But the heart of it still remains. The past and the sense of community, of brotherhood. They came down the street, those young men of Edison, like a unit on patrol, though they were not yet truly soldiers and had no idea what terrible fate of war awaited them. In their matching green jackets, they came, passing by the row homes that decades ago housed the workers who made good money in the factories that now were gone.

They came to let the Zulu Nation and the other gangs know to stay away from the neighborhood and Edison High School.

"Edison Mambo," called out the leaders of this good group of men.

"Olé, Olé," answered his brothers.

Back and forth, they called when they went to the again changed Uptown Theater for *The Great Escape* or an Audie Murphy cowboy movie. Then maybe to a party to do The Twist before heading home. Brothers they were and brothers they are.

"Edison Mambo."

"Olé, Olé."

Now and then. In Life and Death.

Chapter Two

Faculty Interviews

It is fortunate that there are still those who served as faculty members at Edison High School during the Vietnam War. Their personal experiences and observations, while different one from another, help us understand the experiences that the Edison 64 and their classmates took to war.

Following, therefore, are the interviews of:
Dr. Darryrl Johnson;
John Thompson; and
Joanne "Q" Press

FULL CIRCLE

Dr. Darryrl Johnson

I grew up in North Philly with my parents, four brothers, and two sisters. My father was a rifleman in World War II. He was drafted into the U.S. Army and was in France, Germany, and the Philippines, although he never spoke a word about what happened in the war.

My older brother, Lester, was the smartest guy I knew, and I really looked up to him. He graduated from Edison High School and went on to Penn State University because he had a medical deferment. Meanwhile, a lot of his friends got drafted and went to Vietnam. Kind of like my dad, Lester never talked about his situation either.

I wound up at Edison, but not until after bouncing around. First, I went to Elementary School at 17th and Susquehanna and then at 5th and Master, and lastly at Stanton, which was at 18th and Huntington. Next was Gillespie Junior High which was next door to Simon Gratz High School, which I thought would be my next stop.

The School District then did something crazy. I lived at 27th between Susquehanna and Dauphin then. What the District did was divide the street in half so that the kids on the East side of the street went to Edison. The ones on the West side went to Ben Franklin. Both schools were all boys, so you can imagine the rivalry, fights, and craziness that went on right on my own street!

Not only that, but the new boundaries the School District was drawing brought in different gangs from other neighborhoods. The teenage gang members were all too eager for fights, stabbings and what were called, "mass assaults." The gangs were real, the Valley, 15th and Norris, Zulu Nation, and they meant real danger.

I didn't belong to a gang, but there was a lot of what we called "social clubs," which gave us friendship, identity and I guess a kind of protection. I belonged to the Congressional Soul Gents Chapter II which was composed of kids who were a little younger. It also helped me because the social life replaced the fact that I was not going to a co-ed school anymore like I had before Edison.

We'd go to parties and dances instead of fights where we would "battle" with other social clubs like Sophisticated Gents and Delta Soul Gents. My friends in my group were named Cha-Cha, Larry, Lettuce, and Tiny Tim. I was called "Kimba."

The social groups were great. For instance, we'd use one of the fraternity houses on the Temple University campus and put up black lights and have dance-offs. There were even girl groups.

At school, I was an A-B student, but didn't go to class much because of my social life and the gang fights. This all went the only way it could, which was me having to repeat my grade. I was "left down" and my mother was "let down." She was very upset and embarrassed, and I had to give up my social club. What I wanted to do was transfer out of Edison so nobody knew about my problem, but it didn't happen like that. In fact, everything kind of turned out okay.

I learned that my high school was doing away with lunch and dismissing school at 1:05 because of the gang fights. There were a few part-time jobs around though, and I got one at 8th and Columbia, making Phillies Cigars.

Drugs were getting more and more popular and the gangs would actually draft you, so I was glad to have the job for not only the money but for my safety, even though I had to be very careful getting home. Lots of times, I bargained the cigars I got from work for my safety. Also, I was able to get some homework done at the cigar factory.

My home life fell apart as my parents divorced after 27 years of marriage. My father had become an alcoholic and then died in his

50s. The place we were living in was condemned as unsafe by the City, but we had to live there anyway, even with the ceiling collapsing and only partial electricity.

Meanwhile, my mother was working as a domestic in other people's homes and my older brother got married and moved out. Then the City found us another place to live, but it was all the way across town and since I had only had four more months to graduation, I had a lot of commuting to do in addition to everything else.

Edison was really something then, with the gangs still going crazy, and the dropout rate of fifty-percent. There was also the tension from the outside world. We could see the war on television and there were the assassinations. There already was President Kennedy killed in 1963 and Malcolm X in 1965. Then in 1968, Robert Kennedy and Martin Luther King were assassinated, and the turmoil of the civil rights movement grew and grew. It was pretty rough.

Then something great happened to us at Edison or maybe it was just great to us because we were just kids. In 1969, Edison High School won the City Basketball Championship. Led on by our star, Ronnie Thomas' twenty-five points, and Dennis Mathews' 21, we crushed Gratz 93–56 in the Public League semi-final and then with Mathews scoring 22 along with 16 rebounds and Thomas scoring 16, Edison won the league final 69–67.

Our coach, Ed D'Andrea, then took The Edison "Inventors" against Roman Catholic for the coveted City Championship. The title game was held at the famed Palestra on the campus of the University of Pennsylvania. A 10–0 run led by a substitute, Lynn Greer, gave us a 50–44 lead and we held on for a 57–54 win. Everybody in our school felt as proud as could be, and it really made a difference for us, particularly because those of us at Edison who were black, were trying to get racial respect.

Then we started hearing Mr. Glassman on the PA telling us about the Vietnam deaths of our classmates. We would have a moment of silence after each one. It was pretty tough, but not as tough as hearing that our friends were killed in gang warring. I remember to this day when I learned that Bobby Williams, who everybody kind of looked up to, was killed by a shotgun blast. Can you imagine if you've got friends being killed in Vietnam, but then there are people you know getting shot to death right around the block or dying of an overdose?

We wanted to honor our classmates that were killed in the war, so the classes of '71 and '72 came up with the plaque that had their names on it in memory.

So, while this was all going on, there was what was happening to me, I didn't even get a look when I tried out for the basketball team, but I did become a fencer, competing in both sabre and foil. And we won The City Championship twice, and I got to wear a jacket that said that.

My career path was kind of chosen for us at Edison in 10th grade where I was placed in the college prep section. We were the good kids, and the teachers were receptive to us. Still, the war and the draft were going on, so I went into the Air Force, where I got to pick my career of aircraft maintenance specialist.

I first got sent to Lackland Air Force Base in San Antonio, Texas for 8 weeks boot camp in August of 1972. I then had more technical training at Sheppard Air Force Base in Wichita Falls, Texas, which went back to 1941 when it was the U.S. Army Air Corp Training Center. It became the home of more extra technical training than any other base in the Air Education and Training Command.

Then my bouncing around started up again. After Lackland and Sheppard, I went to Plattsburg Air Force base in New York. It was the oldest military base in the U.S., going back to 1814. It was also on Lake Champlain, twenty miles from Canada, which meant it was cold.

Then I got my orders to go to Thailand, but the Peace Agreement got signed. This got me sent to McGuire Air Force Base in New Jersey where I became a flight engineer which was fortunate because I loved working with jets.

By now, I was married with two great kids and flying to places like Spain and Iceland, delivering supplies. Then after 1978, I worked out of the Navy Yard in South Philly until 1996. I had earned my B.A. at Temple University in 1990, and as the Navy Yard was going to close, Temple had a program called "Cite" to cross-train us to be teachers.

The Navy Yard did close in 1996, but I was fortunate to do two more years with the U.S. Navy, so by then, I had my twenty-five years, and I started my search for a teaching job.

Who would have guessed that this would take me back to Edison where I hadn't set foot in 27 years? Even so, some of the faculty who had taught me, such as Mr. Porter, the Chairman of the Math Department helped me. I became a member of the math department and taught at Edison for 17 years, during which I earned my doctorate and had a new family after I divorced and remarried.

One thing I made sure to do was to make sure the students learned about Vietnam. The plaque was still at Edison, and we had an annual Memorial Ceremony with a candle lighting, which I became responsible for. I also was the proposer for The Historic Marker placed by the Pennsylvania Historical and Museum Commission in 2014, so there will always be a reminder of those who served and sacrificed.

The marker reads, "Sixty-four former Edison students died in service to their country during the Vietnam War between 1965 and 1971, more than any school in the nation. These young men represent the burden and disparity of the war on poor rural and urban communities throughout America. Whether they enlisted voluntarily or were assigned draft numbers that they were unable to avoid by deferment, these men made the ultimate sacrifice."

I am still active at Edison and am serving as the historian of the Edison 64 and emcee of the annual Memorial Day celebration. I am honored to be doing it.

THE OTHER WAY AROUND

John Thompson

I went from Vietnam to Edison High School. The other way around from most, you could say, but for certain, it helped me help a lot of students.

Even though I was in my third year as a student at Temple University, I found myself facing the draft. I tried for a deferment, but then I enlisted in the United States Air Force. This meant more time to serve of course, but I would have the opportunity of being more than a "grunt."

I did my basic training in San Antonio, Texas and then got sent for advanced training in Denver where I learned about weapons systems. I was the oldest and most educated guy there, which had its plusses and minuses.

My last deployment in the U.S. was at Wright Patterson Air Force Base in Ohio. I kept learning more about airplanes and technical things, even classified material, which I enjoyed, and I got to take college courses at Wright University.

Then it was time to go overseas. I was stationed at Guam for a while, where I even got to earn some more college credits, this time at the University of Guam. Next came the war which for me meant Saigon and mostly, Da Nang. There was an Air Force Base there. It was divided into USAF and the Army and Da Nang City where you weren't allowed unless you went in good-sized groups.

I tried to make friends with the Vietnamese, who we called, "The Natives," which wasn't easy because their families were often broken up and it was sometimes hard to tell the good guys from the bad ones.

It was also rough because of the usual craziness of any war, which meant getting shot at and so on. Also, there was some serious racial friction between our own people.

My last year in Nam was pretty much a lot of hell, so I was glad to be sent back to the States where I was advised not to wear my uniform in public because of the anti-war stuff going on. When I got home, I went back to Temple University to finish my degree while I worked at my father's trucking company, doing paperwork. He had been at that company for a long time so that when I was a kid, we lived at 4500 Mulberry Street which was a corner property, so we were thought to be well-to-do. I grew up with my sister, Merrilyn, and my mom, Katherine, was a homemaker.

My girlfriend was a teacher. Her name was Velda, and she and I got married. She would talk about how difficult the students could be, which made it a challenge for me, so I started working as a substitute teacher at Gillespie Junior High.

Then the principal asked me to report to the Vocational Office for an interview because I had made some changes which were good for the kids. Even though I was thinking about going back into engineering which I found to be challenging and important in the Air Force, I met with two people who talked to me about teaching.

They asked me to try a position at Edison High in North Philly which was neither close to or as nice as where I was living, which was near Frankford High School. But I reported to Edison where I met with Principal Al Glassman and Vocational Department Head Ed Chilician. Then I met with the other members of the Department.

I started my career at Edison by being taken to a dingy "hole in the wall," which was to be my classroom and shop. The two other teachers made it clear that they felt I was there to take their jobs.

My hole in the wall came equipped with very little and no lesson plan. In addition, I was not even allowed into the tool room to have anything to work with. So, there I was with 15 "behavior" kids and some batteries.

When I discussed with my fiancé the fact that in addition, all my students were black in a racially mixed school, Velda told me that "now you're seeing it for what it really is." I decided to do something about it.

Although I hadn't discussed my military experience with anybody, I began telling my students about body bags, soldiers with maggots and picking up a corpse that came apart. I wanted them to know what the grown-up world could be like.

I had one student who was really big and could be very difficult sometimes. Once he was about to swing at me, I grabbed him by the ear. He went to the principal about me and Mr. Glassman said, "You can't treat my boys like that."

I answered that I gave three years of my life getting shot at, and I won't be disrespected like that, that my students were young men, not boys, and I wanted to meet with the student's father. When I did meet with him, he asked me why I didn't kick his son's behind and gave me the "go ahead" next time.

As the school year went on, I got more equipment, even at my own expense. The students did better and better and the reputation of my vocational program grew. Representatives from big companies, like Mr. Duke Yeakel of Bell Telephone and others came to meet with me.

I respected those kids, who were supposed to be behavioral problems, and they respected me. I believed in a holistic program of both academic and technical and that the program should be 8 to 5.

Things were good and bad as they went on during my 45 years at Edison. The young men were often ready for good jobs when they finished my program, instead of standing on the corner or flunking out of college. We had a real Academy of Applied Electrical Science which was founded in 1969 as a partnership with industry.

Still, there was the gang wars in the neighborhood and the War was still going on in Vietnam. It was heartbreaking to hear the names of our Edison boys who were killed in Vietnam. "You don't know what hell is," I would tell my students, describing what I could about the War. I wanted them to know everything I could teach them, for they were really like my sons.

"Q"

Joanne Press

My name is JoAnne Press, and I was born and raised in the Kensington section of Philadelphia. My family's name was "McHugh," which I kept until I got married so that for many of the years I was at Edison, I was known as "Miss McHugh" and often referred to by my students as "Q."

I lived with my parents and my sister, Madeleine. My neighborhood was good and even had a nice park called, "Norris Square" although it started getting not so nice after a while because of the drunks and vagrants in the park. Then we weren't allowed to go through there on our way to and from school.

Norris Square eventually got so bad that in the 1980s, it was called "Needle Park." Fortunately, community groups started getting involved, and Norris Square is now an award-winning green space that would make William Penn, who deeded it to Isaac Norris in 1863, as proud as he should be.

I was educated at St. Basil Academy which is a Catholic all-girls school founded in 1931 in the Fox Chase area of Philadelphia. After graduating from there, I went to Notre Dame of Maryland where I majored in Biology and took a minor in English. My college was the first four-year Roman Catholic College for Women in the United States.

My plan was to work in Baltimore doing scientific research after I graduated. However, my dear dad passed away. As it was just my mother and sister in Philadelphia, I returned to help.

When I came back, I looked for jobs in research, but the only thing I could come up with was at Hires Rootbeer. Unfortunately, it wasn't at all the job for me.

What was fortunate was that my sister suggested that I take some credits in education so that I could do substitute teaching. I went to Temple University which enabled me to substitute in various junior high schools, and in September of 1962, I found myself at Edison High School, which was a mostly black, all-boys school in North Philadelphia.

Madeleine was much against it, but I told myself that I would give it a three-week try. I met and liked the principal, Dr. Robert Wayne Clarke, and the students. I also earned my Master's Degree in the Psychology of Reading from Temple University in 1965. And then those three weeks turned into forty-two years!

I started in the Science Department, and after a dozen years or so, I switched to the English Department. Sometimes, I even taught math. In all my courses, I used my skill and experience in teaching, which was often greatly needed. In one case, for instance, I had a student who was reading at the pre-primer level, which meant he really couldn't read at all. But we worked together, and he progressed.

It was not all easy. We were poorly equipped. I often had as many as 55 students, many sitting in the window sills and sharing books that were horribly outdated.

However, I did well, and we got along. I loved my students, and they followed my rules, such as raising your hand before speaking and not getting up and walking around. They also respected my firm but fair rules about using the hall pass.

My success with my students is most likely attributable to three sources. First, my mother was stern and believed in fair rules and discipline. Secondly, I truly believe that I have been bestowed with empathy so that I always tried to consider the feelings and needs of each person in my class. Lastly, was our principal, Dr. Robert Wayne Clarke. Principal Clarke was firm, helpful and loving. He correctly assessed me when I began at Edison by telling me, "You're really green, aren't you?" He believed that we should all follow the rules, and at the end of every day, he said over the public-address system, "We love you, boys."

I am happy now as I remember my forty-two years at Edison and how I shared the beliefs of Dr. Clarke. I am also deeply saddened when I think of our students who proudly went off to the Vietnam War and either came back suffering from the trauma of the war. Or not at all.

Chapter Three

The War

"Now we have a problem in trying to make our power credible and Vietnam looks like the place."
President John F. Kennedy

"The Vietnam War was a great tragedy for our country."
Henry Kissinger

The Vietnam War, also known as "The American War," "The War Against the Americans to Save the Nation," "The Resistance Against America War," and "The Second Indo-China War," was as complicated as its name. It involved France, Japan, Germany, Britain, Russia, China, Cambodia, Laos, Australia, New Zealand, South Vietnam, North Vietnam, North Korea, South Korea, Cuba, Khmer Republic, Khmer Rouge, Viet Cong and the Philippines.

While all wars generally have two sides, this war was a historical and geopolitical kaleidoscope, which it is fair to say began in 1847 when the French sent its ships supposedly to protect the Christian population against Emperor Gialong. The intended results were accomplished some three decades later when Vietnam came under the control of France, something Vietnam suffered deeply as it had endured the colonization of the Chinese Han Dynasty from 111 BC until its victory and freedom nearly a thousand years later at the Battle of Bach Dang River in 938.

The modern colonization expanded when the French occupation was joined by Japan's invasion of 9/22/40. This resulted in the Vichy French and the Imperial Japanese occupying Vietnam until March 1945 when Japan imprisoned the French. Then came the entry of members of the United States OSS and on September 2, 1945, the Declaration of Independence of the Democratic Republic of Vietnam by Ho Chi Minh, who had previously met with the OSS and even as far back as President Woodrow Wilson, had reached out for U.S. acceptance.

One would have thought that this would have brought at least a positive relationship between Vietnam and the United States. However, what happened was rather, continued distrust and acts of self-interest. President Truman, for instance, repeatedly ignored Ho Chi Minh's request for recognition and further authorized aircraft and $15,000,000 in military aid to the post-war French, whom he wished would act as an agent of the United States.

The aspirations of France, aided by the United States, including the assistance provided by President Eisenhower in his Saigon Military Mission, failed. Rather, what prevailed was the historic battle of Dien Bien Phu in which 40,000 Viet Minh, as the independent Vietnamese referred to themselves, soundly defeated the contingent of 15,000 French, by General Giap's use of heavy artillery. The victory by the Viet Minh on May 7, 1954, effectively ended what is known as The First Indo China War, which lasted from 1946 to 1954 in which Vietnam was divided at the 17th parallel by the Geneva Accords.

During this time, The Korean War was raging from 1950 to 1953. Beginning with the invasion of 75,000 North Korean troops, this conflagration became a battle between East versus West, in which a woefully unprepared United States and the United Nations engaged North Korea, Communist Chinese, and the USSR.

The results were staggering, including the loss of 1.3 million lives, the enmity between North Korea and the United States, which poses a global threat even today, and the "Domino Theory" espoused by President Eisenhower, who had led the U.S .and its Allies to victory in World War II. That theory as stated in his historic news conference, became the rallying-call, if not the reasoning for our long-standing position. On April 7, 1954, he stated, "You have a row of dominoes set up, you knock over the first one and what will happen to the last one is a certainty that it will go over very quickly." It was therefore, partly for the belief in an alleged salvation of Indochina, Burma, Indonesia, and even Japan, that the blood and death of the Vietnam War came upon us.

By the time President Kennedy defeated Richard Nixon in 1960, the Vietnam confrontation had expanded. JFK was not committed to introducing combat troops to South East Asia, or so he espoused, but neither was he satisfied with clandestine CIA operations and military advisors. In any case, there were more than 15,000 U.S. troops deployed in Vietnam by the time President Kennedy was assassinated and the Viet Cong and North Vietnam had committed even greater numbers.

On taking office, President Johnson was neither committed to nor knowledgeable of the scale of our involvement in Vietnam. Two days after taking office, however, he pledged "Strength and determination in battling Communism." This was so as LBJ's primary interest in U.S. domestic policies allowed the continuation of the intentions of Robert McNamara, et al, who held over from the Kennedy administration.

On August 4, 1964, two U.S. ships, the Maddox and the Turner Joy were allegedly attacked in the Gulf of Tonkin by North Vietnamese torpedo boats. This led to Congress's approval of "The Gulf of Tonkin Resolution" which gave President Johnson the power and the right to launch a full-scale war in Vietnam without further Congressional approval. A massive escalation of U.S. troops resulted. Despite passionate protests at home, there were 200,000 U.S. troops deployed by December 1965 and a total of 500,000 military personnel by 1969.

The Vietnam War itself continued to be divisive and confusing. Our military correctly claimed that they never lost a battle. Even the enemy's Tet Offensive was a losing effort in the field. However, the explosion of television coverage brought the horror of war to our living rooms and dinner tables. No one will forget the image of the Buddhist Monk, Thick Quang Duc, setting himself on fire, or the naked Vietnamese child, Phan-Thi Phuoc, fleeing napalm bombs in June of 1972, or the famous execution photo in which General Nguyen Ngoc Luan executed a Viet Cong prisoner with a pistol shot to his head.

Divisiveness and trouble were also disturbing our Country at home. There was the union and entanglement of the anti-war sentiment with the nation's racial discord which led to riots breaking out at the Democratic National Convention in Chicago in 1968. Walter Cronkite, our nation's wise elder had pronounced to us that the War was unwinnable, and four Kent State Students were shot to death by our own National Guard.

All of this was despite the belief by our generals and president that two more weeks of the bombing of North Vietnam would lead to the victory of the United States instead of the Fall of Saigon on April 30, 1975.

And what is the end result of all of this? What was bought with the death of 2,000,000 civilians, 1,100,000 enemies, 250,000 South Vietnam soldiers and more than 58,000 United States troops including the 64 young men from Edison High School?

There were many, many more, who never forgot, who served and suffered injuries to their bodies and their minds and to their hearts.

The suffering will go on until all those who served, and their families, are all dead. Our soldiers and their families are still scarred and ruined. Yet there are now five-star hotels in Saigon and excellent "deals" on travel. "Must see" tours and tens of billions and dollars of Vietnam imports and exports. This must not be the heritage of the service, the sacrifice, and the suffering.

CHAPTER FOUR

The War at Home

The end of World War II is best remembered by that famous photograph of the sailor kissing the dental assistant in her white dress at Times Square on August 14, 1945. There were tons of ticker tape and parades to celebrate Japan's surrender. The vets were heroes.

They were heroes, not "baby killers." And our Country welcomed them back with hugs and salutes instead of spitting on them. Even now, some fifty years later, the servicemen of Vietnam receive little acceptance, let alone honor, as the interviews of the Edison soldiers make it clear. For instance, when I asked these fine men if the people around them knew of their service, there was very little positive response. Only one or two told me that somebody in the neighborhood knew that they were "in 'Nam" or "the war."

This is not to say that there have not been attempts to salute the sacrifices many gave, such as the Vietnam Veterans Memorial in Washington, D.C., a similar but smaller Philadelphia Vietnam Veterans Memorial, and other similar gestures such as the naming of a street for the Edison 64, the Pennsylvania Marker, and the annual memorial service at Edison High. These, however, are more it seems, to touch the hearts of the servicemen and women and their families, rather than to express the feelings of a proud or even appreciative society.

On May 25, 2012, President Barack Obama issued a proclamation commemorating "the 50th Anniversary of the Vietnam War." In doing so, he called on federal, state, and local officials to honor the Vietnam Veterans from May 28, 2012, to November 11, 2015. Now, thanks to the bill signed into law by President Trump, March 29 is National Vietnam War Veterans Day every year. However, one may seriously question whether is it not more likely than not, that the present splits between political and social groups and the appearance of aggressive demonstrators will mean that the annual March 29 holiday will be marred by anti-war and anti-government demonstrations.

Was the Vietnam War so different from wars before or since? Why are we neither shocked nor surprised by the lingering, hateful and disgraceful attitude towards those who gave of themselves. A brief examination of our history shows similar behavior in the past which has somehow been forgotten.

Perhaps the greatest cause of domestic anti-war feeling during the Vietnam conflict was in response to the re-introduction of the military draft. There were marches, burning of draft cards and of the American flag, and song after song, from Phil Ochs, "I Ain't Marching Anymore" to "Where Are You Now My Son?" by Joan Baez.

Such anti-American, unpatriotic actions are not new to our country. The New York Draft Riots of July 13–16, 1863 were a ferocious and deadly response to President Lincoln's actions to bolster Union troops by conscription, but at the same time, allowing those who were rich enough, to avoid the draft by paying a fee. This resulted in the transformation of anti-draft riots into attacks on blacks by predominantly Irish immigrants. More than a hundred people were killed, churches, homes, public buildings and even an orphanage were burned down.

In addition, there was large-scale "draft dodging," a strong anti-war political movement, protests, and a split in the Democratic Party. Of course, there were many songs then, such as "Drafted into the Army," and "Tenting on the Old Campground." The most memorable anti-war creation is *The Red Badge of Courage* by Stephen Crane, which though published after the Civil War was concluded, most accurately describes the ugliness of war in an unforgettable and lasting fashion despite the fact that the author had no experience in the field at all.

The Vietnam War is also similar to preceding American conflicts in its interweaving of anti-war sentiment with other protests and anti-institutional behavior. As described above, the Civil War and racial animus were often inseparable. Similarly, there were racial conflicts in World War I such as when nineteen African-American soldiers who had engaged in armed mutiny, were executed. This had an effect on both black support of the war and of their own assertive actions.

More involved in the growth of our society was the effect of Dr. Martin Luther King on both the Vietnam War and the Civil Rights Movement. On April 4, 1967, Dr. King delivered a powerful anti-war speech in front of the thousands who packed the Riverside Church in New York. The speech, "A Time to Break Silence," condemned President Johnson and violence against the Vietnamese. This caused public outcry against Dr. King by his own constituency and the public at large. "Peace and civil rights don't mix," he said in quoting his detractors. Similarly, he addressed the relationship between poverty and racism and even spoke of the suffering of our enemy in the War. "I think of them, too, because it is clear to me that there will be no meaningful solution there until some attempt is made to know them and their broken cries."

The preaching of Dr. King and his fiery commitment to Christian belief did much to advocate for peace and non-violence. In doing so, he also issued an impassioned call by word and action for the anti-war and civil rights movements to come together. In doing so, he stirred the passion of both movements.

It should be noted that in a like fashion, the striving for women's equality came together with the anti-war movement. One must acknowledge the actions of such groups as the Women's International League for Peace and Freedom and of individuals such as Congresswoman Bella Abzug, who was also a founder of Women Strike for Peace. Similarly, religious movements such as the Quakers, Seventh-day Adventists, and Mennonites remained committed to their pacifism.

While racist discord, civil rights, women's rights, and non-violence were all causing differences of opinion and conflict that affected the public attitudes about the Vietnam War and our soldiers, there were other movements that caused social schisms, increased tension, and civil disruption. As mentioned earlier, there was the everyday violence caused by the warring of more than a hundred gangs in the Philadelphia area alone. There also was the increased growth of anarchist groups such as Abbie Hoffman's Yippies, the anti-institutional SDS or "Students for a Democratic Society" and the lawless Black Panthers, who occupied Columbia University at gunpoint, and the Symbionese Liberation Army which featured millionaire, Patty Hearst.

All these factors swirled together like a cyclone so that there was no peace, no unanimity, no harmony. Small differences became large differences, became crevasses that could not be bridged. At the same time, the perception of reality and therefore reality itself, underwent a profound change as the number of households with televisions went from under 10% to over 90%.

Television brought the Vietnam War to everyone's home. As media master, Marshall McLuhan stated, "Vietnam was lost in the living rooms of America, not on the battlefields of Vietnam."

Death and combat were shown daily as were anti-war demonstrations. Further, as Erin Mc Laughlin has observed in her "TV Coverage of the Vietnam War and the Vietnam Veteran," television news dramatically changed the frame of the war after the Tet Offensive. Images of the U.S. led massacre at My Lai dominated television, yet the daily atrocities committed by North Vietnam and the Viet Cong rarely made the evening news. Moreover, the anti-war movement at home gained increasing media attention while the U.S. soldier was forgotten.

CHAPTER FIVE

They Served and Survived

It has been my honor to have met with numerous alumni of Edison High School who served in the Vietnam War. I was put in touch with them by Dr. Darryrl Johnson, Historian of the Edison 64. He provided me with a list of servicemen who had attended various Edison or Veterans events. This was a most valuable asset as many of the Edison alumni who served in Vietnam had been killed in action or died of natural causes in the 50 years that had passed. Fortunately, most of those I contacted, agreed to be interviewed.

We sat in their parlors and in their kitchens, and on their front porches. Most were in the North Philly section of the City, but whether we were there, or elsewhere, the reception I received was always cordial, even though palpable tension was imminent.

My hosts would invariably meet me wearing some part of their uniform or mementos, such as hats, shirts, buttons, most frequently something with "Edison 64" on them. Often, my hosts would have photos or printed material about their unit, "The History of the 173rd" or the like. I always wore a necktie and carried my briefcase in which there was the necessary yellow legal pad and pens.

I would be offered a bottle of water or a soft drink and introduced to whatever family members were around. Then the veterans let me get to know them. I would ask where they grew up, which almost always was North Philadelphia, although in my first interview that place was a Nazi prison camp. Then we talked about their families, who usually were like any other. Like most people in the "City of Brotherly Love," they grew up in row houses and knew their neighbors. Both were comforting.

Then we talked about elementary school where the big thing was whether you got to go home in the middle of the day for lunch, and then junior high before going to Edison. Almost universally, the men I spoke with liked their high school experience which of course, included girls and a wide variety of sports including football, track, and basketball but surprisingly, also fencing and swimming.

Most important to them, was the feeling of camaraderie which it seems to me, was fostered by the neighborhood and their school. "Edison Mambo" was the chant of the young men as they left their neighborhood to go to the Uptown Theater, a dance party or to Center City. And there was the tradition that all newcomers must kiss the backsides of the stone lions that stood outside the school.

But equally common to the experience of young men, became the scarcity of paying jobs, both while students or after graduation. The lucky kids might get a job at the local grocery store or the lumber yard in the neighborhood, but as far as anything that could be of real help, like at a factory or the like, there was very little opportunity. The unemployment rate in North Philadelphia was twenty percent and the average income was slightly better than $3,000 per year.

At the same time, gang warfare was a real and dangerous element which included everything from "beat-downs" to bloody battles with chains and pipes, to killings, be it with knives, makeshift firearms, called "zip guns," which were most often fashioned from auto aerials. There also were pistols and shotguns. Even staying "close to home" was no guarantee of safety because there were armed invasions and confrontations brought about by the mixing of gangs at Edison High School. The danger posed by the gangs was so great, that rather than have a melee and killing in the cafeteria, the school day ended at 1 PM.

Next, we came to discussions of how my hosts got into the service. Most of the Edison alumni enlisted, to secure a paycheck and avoid the gangs. They did so often without telling their parents first. As you might imagine, the reactions at home were largely disapproving, sometimes dramatically so.

Leaving home for "the service" after the swearing-in at 401 N. Broad Street was always dramatic, whether it was because the family somehow participated or the new servicemen were on a train with equally nervous strangers. I listened to the Edison vets tell me about their first experience in Vietnam, which was the intolerably oppressive heat and usually the acrid and unforgettable odor of burning human waste. Sometimes, the first experiences were even more indelible, like landing and deplaning right in the middle of a firefight.

The length of our time together in those parlors and on those porches, was usually an hour and a half to two hours. By the halfway point, those heroes who served our Country a half-century ago, would usually be almost overwhelmed. There were also recollections of lasting friendships, near-miracles, and comedy to be sure. But there was also the confirmation of long-held and unforgettable horror and terror.

We talked through that and to their discharge and life after the service, but what I heard, what I was honored to have shared with me, was always so moving, so dramatic, that I had to sit in my car for twenty minutes or so before trying to drive. Men telling me that they enlisted because of JFK's speech, "Ask not...," that they heard on the bus or the terror of being attacked while they slept in their foxhole in the bush, or how they were still suffering with guilt because they had been unharmed. And how they were spit on when they came home and had nightmares every night for fifty years, and that our Country killed all its scout dogs and how the neighbors of the Edison heroes knew nothing about what they have given for us. How our Edison heroes had cancers and rotting limbs and skin diseases that didn't heal and that it took them 25 years for the Veteran's Administration to give them their benefits.

I have tried my best to pass on what was given to me and to share the emotions and tone. You will note that each interview is absent the name of the Edison veteran I met with in order to protect their privacy. There also is however, a separate alphabetical list of those whom I've interviewed, so they are given due credit for their service, courage, and grace.

I will never forget any of what I heard. I hope you, too, will always remember what these soldiers of Edison have told us.

INTERVIEWS IN ALPHABETICAL ORDER

George Bembischew
Dave Bernhardt
Lenny Booker
Jeremiah Candelaria
James Douglas
Wilfredo Gonzalez
Brian Griffin
Darryl Hairston
Leonard Hitch
Flint Jackson

Peter Jackson
Lee Johnson
Gerald Jones
David Lightsey
Lawrence Mack
Serafin Natal
Norbert Pirela
Delano Stones
Gene Tatum
Stefan Boyd Williams

SURVIVOR INTERVIEWS

Not in alphabetical order for anonymity

1. Beautiful and Terrible
2. My Partner
3. Bad Times, Bad Times
4. Messed Up
5. Ghost Job
6. Thirteen Cents
7. Smiley
8. Twenty More Years
9. E and E
10. Poetry
11. Three Golden Rules
12. Rocket City
13. My Legs
14. June Bug
15. POW to Paratrooper
16. Nightmare
17. "Pete"
18. Bittersweet
19. My Escape
20. The Watch

BEAUTIFUL AND TERRIBLE

I lived in West Philadelphia until I was 7. It was a very social place at 5700 Vine Street where I grew up, and I was always playing in the street with other kids. I had two sisters and a brother, although Gertrude passed.

We moved to North Philly, which led me to Stokely Elementary School, Vaux Jr. High and when the time came, Edison High School. Most importantly, I was in the Boy Scouts, Troop 536, which I attribute to my father, who went to Drexel University and was an electrical engineer. This gave me a great love and appreciation for nature and science. I still remember my Gilbert Chemistry set!

I also liked the military from when I was young because I had relatives, both men and women, who served all the way back to the Civil War, where my great, great grandfather's company received the Congressional Medal of Honor.

I also liked to fish in salt and fresh water, including in New Jersey, and along the Philadelphia Airport where you could get your bait right there. I caught lots, including bass to crabs, and I had tropical fish at home. I liked it so much, in fact, I still fish at Ridge and Midvale in Philly, and in Jersey, and the Poconos.

In high school, I liked my teachers and science classes, not that everything was perfect. In fact, I did get in trouble with some of the other kids, but I fought back. Then you said, "I give," and it was over.

Again, overall my school experience was pretty good. I ran long distance in track and cross-country. I also won an art scholarship for my drawings and photos. During this time, my mom was a school teacher, and my dad worked for the federal government. So once again, I had it pretty good, particularly when I met Annette, who became my wife.

Because I liked the military and service and science fiction so much, I enlisted in the Air Force, which was because I particularly liked airplanes. I was so eager to serve, I enlisted before I graduated and stayed overseas until 1969. I then stayed on at Maguire Air Force Base until 1978.

Meanwhile, my wife, who went to Bok High School, and I did also for a while, enlisted in the Army. She went into intelligence and volunteered for Vietnam twice. She eventually came into the War through Saigon and served five or six years. When she was done, she came home as an E-6, but much to my sadness died from exposure to Agent Orange.

My own military career was varied. I did my basic at Lackland Airforce Base in San Antonio, Texas. Then I was at Holloman Air Force Base in New Mexico which had joined with the White Sands Proving Ground. I worked with fuels and in Special Operations, but I did not like it at all and volunteered for Vietnam to get away from there.

I entered Vietnam through Saigon and was under fire from the first minute I was there. It was all lit up as we approached. All the lights went out, and we hit the ground running with our weapons out. Our plane received numerous bullet holes.

Afterwards, I did a lot of moving around as my unit would go with the 366th Tactical Air Wing, which became the Air Combat Command, and we'd go back and forth to Holloman, then Nam, and back and forth. I also spent a lot of time with the 82nd Air Borne and the ROK, the South Korean Marines, who were very tough. We would go out together to recover downed pilots and the "black boxes" and fuel samples from our aircraft.

While I was in Vietnam, or "in country" as we called it, I saw nature that was as beautiful as I ever saw or even imagined. There were the rivers, the canals, the mountains, the beaches and the flora and fauna from rhododendron to tigers and almost 1,000 species of birds.

But as beautiful as it was, it also was just as terrible like when my friend, Nate, from home, got killed. Nate Washington and I knew each other from the neighborhood and school and worked together in a coal yard at 28th and York. And we went to Saigon together. It was there that he was killed while he slept by an infiltrator with a blowgun who sent a dart through his sleeping bag.

I don't think it ended right for any of us. I know it didn't for me. While I came home alive, I was disabled from damage to my heart and back. There was no "coming home" party. Rather, people were calling us "baby killers" instead of celebrating what we did for our Country and others.

One special thing worth remembering remained with me. Me and my buddies were on our backs in the jungle. We all felt we were being watched which is not a very good thing. Then somebody in my unit said, "Look up," which we did and there was a giant Buddha overlooking us and when we saw it, we knew that we were going to be okay. This feeling of security still comes and goes, but at least I can feel those special times when I was back in the Boy Scouts, the time of the Great Buddha, and when I am with my son.

MY PARTNER

I came to the United States when I was fourteen, the youngest in my family. My parents and brothers and sisters were already here. We lived in a second-floor apartment at Germantown Avenue and Westmoreland. My dad worked in New York City at a record store and came to Philly on the weekends to be with us. He moved here in 1962 and opened his own music store, "*Centro Musical.*"

I started school at St. Stephen's, which was hard for me because I hadn't learned English that well. Then I transferred to Roman Catholic and eventually to Edison for 11th and 12th grades. My English was better then, so I liked Edison best and liked to play on the roof and football. I graduated in 1965 and my brother the year before.

After school, I'd go and help my dad in his record store, which I really enjoyed because I liked music so much, particularly Hector Lavoe and the Fania All-Stars.

Hector Lavoe came to the United States like I did and performed first with Roberto Garcia's band and then as a soloist with Willie Colon. He had a lot of hits like *El Malo*. The Fania All-Stars were at the top of salsa for more than forty years and Hector sometimes appeared with them.

My plan was to go to college after high school, but I got one of those letters that said I was drafted. There was nothing I could do about it, so on February 8, 1966, I reported to 401 N. Broad Street where I had my physical and filled out a lot of papers like all the other guys. There we were told we could go home temporarily, but we had to report in two weeks.

So, when the time came, I joined a large number of other recruits and got on the train. I think it was at the North Philadelphia station and off we went. It was crazy. Nobody knew what was going to happen. Some guys even jumped off the train.

Everything was a blur. I do remember that when we got to our destination, there was a band playing to welcome us. But right after that, we were all taken into a room and a tough-looking guy told us, "You have nothing now!" We all felt lost.

I got orders to go to Fort Hood, Texas, which was over 200,000 acres and midway between Austin and Waco. I did my basic there and my AIT, Advanced Infantry Training, as well.

My new family was the 2nd Armored Division. Our motto was, "Hell on Wheels." I earned my licenses to drive trucks, jeeps, personnel carriers, and tanks. Imagine that. I'm 19 years old and here I am driving a tank. They also gave us training in evading capture which was a good thing because if you got caught during training, they tied you up and gave you a hard time.

My time at Fort Hood didn't have too many bad parts. I made friends with two guys from back home, Norman Sugarman from Philly and Arthur Fallon from Ardmore. The food was okay, except on Thursday when they served us liver. And I got promoted to Specialist, E-4 and then I got new orders and off I went to Fort Benning, Georgia, which was on the Alabama-Georgia border.

Fort Benning was the home of the Infantry School and such famous soldiers as George C. Marshall and Dwight Eisenhower, who later became President. Its motto was, "One Force, One Fight." And it also contained the Armor School Airborne School, and Scout Dog School, which I knew nothing about, but which changed my life forever.

When I got to Fort Benning, they taught me all about Military Working Dogs, or "War Dogs," which are scout dogs. We were called "scouts" and "handlers." Except for Labrador Retrievers which were used to silently follow blood trails, all the 4,000 dogs that served in Vietnam were German or Belgian Shepherds, and they did everything else from going into tunnels, doing water patrol, and protecting our perimeter.

There were 28 of us training to be dog handlers. We were assigned a dog and divided into smaller groups. It was not unusual that the dog had worked with another handler before us, so we were the ones really getting the training.

My dog was a big black and tan German Shepherd named Arias. Together we worked on communications. The commands, "Sit, stay" and so on were given by silent hand gestures. Unfortunately, Arias was not at all cooperative, so I had to start over with another dog. He was all black and because he was very smart, I was able to catch-up with the other handlers and dogs very quickly.

After three months of very rough training, including all kinds of terrain and battle conditioning, the 43rd Infantry Scout Division, including me, headed off to Vietnam. We took everything we needed in our four-engine cargo planes. This included our duffle bags, dogs, jeeps, and weapons. Our first stop was California, then Guam, Wake Island, Philippines, Hawaii, and lastly, we arrived in Saigon.

As we landed in Vietnam, our captain warned us that we were landing in a combat area, so we had to be ready for anything. What we got was something we couldn't prepare for and that was a big jet being loaded with casket after casket. I'll never forget that.

We stayed for two days in Saigon which was supposed to be unbearably hot, but our stops along the way there had gotten steadily warmer, so in a way we were ready for it. Then we went to Bearcat Base which is where the dog kennels were. And in less than a week, we were about our missions.

These missions were "Search and Destroy," which means life or death. Anything that moved, it was your duty to take it out. So, everything was tension or suffering. The pressure on me was and still is, unbelievable because as a sergeant, I was in charge of a squad, which was usually about ten men.

We always went in pairs and as dog handlers, we had our German Shepherds with us. Wherever we were needed, that's where we went, even to the Green Berets. As a scout and platoon leader, I would be in the lead or "take the point" and you never knew what was waiting for you. Without my canine partner who could sense things, I had no idea what was waiting for us. There was no way I would have survived.

We would be out in combat for a week to ten days and then back to base for two. In some ways, those two days in camp made what we had to do even harder because, in some crazy way, you were so involved in the ambushes, the explosions, the killings, that you somehow got used to it, even though you knew it was changing you inside and that you'd never be the same.

I went from one place of terror and death to another for ten months. It was war every day and trying to sleep in the jungle or rice paddies every night with horrible sounds all around and explosions. Two things, though, were a comfort. Number one was my dog was with me, my partner. And number two, no matter how heavy the incoming fire and shelling was, I never got hit.

That's not to say I wasn't hurt. I've got lots of wounds, inside and out. And the PTSD, which almost all of us got, that's still here. And I had to fight and fight with the VA for my benefits. Even though every day is rough, I would do it again because I love this Country.

I am also very fortunate to have a wonderful family and two dogs I got when I came home. That's a big help.

But one more thing, all of us who were dog handlers wanted to bring our animal partners home when our tour was done. We were even willing to buy them. The government told us no, that our dogs were the property of the United States Government. No way were they just property. They risked their lives for us and protected us, like one day I was at the point and I let the captain know there was an ambush ahead, and he tells me there isn't. So, we go out again and the captain sees my dog stop still as a stone and then move his left ear. What I reported was accepted and all kinds of air power was called in and what got blown to pieces proved we were right.

So, we were true partners, my dog and me. We shared a bond. We were family, and I miss him every day and just cannot accept that thousands of our dogs were killed by my government or given to the Vietnamese who considered them a delicacy. None of our canine heroes came home.

Author's Addendum
The Betrayal of the Most Loyal

Dogs have been used in warfare as far back as 700 BC, serving many useful purposes for the Egyptians, Greeks, Britons, Romans, Ephesians, and Persians.

Over four thousand dogs served in the Vietnam War. Most were Shepherds, but several were black Labradors and some mixed breeds. They worked as sentries, explosive detectors, fighters, scouts, and loyal companions. Their sense and loyalty were unquestionable and as valuable in Vietnam as in World War I, World War II, and Korea.

But despite their value and goodness, and the fact that the dog and his handler had the third greatest mortality rate by job description, exceeded only by pilots and snipers, these heroic war dogs were treated in such a way that can only be described as sickening.

While it is widely estimated that our canine soldiers saved an estimated 10,000 lives, their reward was being slaughtered. Unlike during our other wars, they were not permitted to return home when their tours were done. They were treated as only surplus equipment. As such, they were euthanized, killed by the armed services they served, or given to the South Vietnamese for food.

President Clinton stepped in some twenty-five years later and signed "Robby's Law" allowing for the adoption of the dogs by their handlers. Unfortunately, House Law 5314 became law not only after the dog after whom it was named was dead, but further, the legislation was easily circumvented, often by the black market so that it was not until 2016 when President Obama signed the National Defense Authorization Act, that the shameful and hideous practice of killing our canine soldiers was barred.

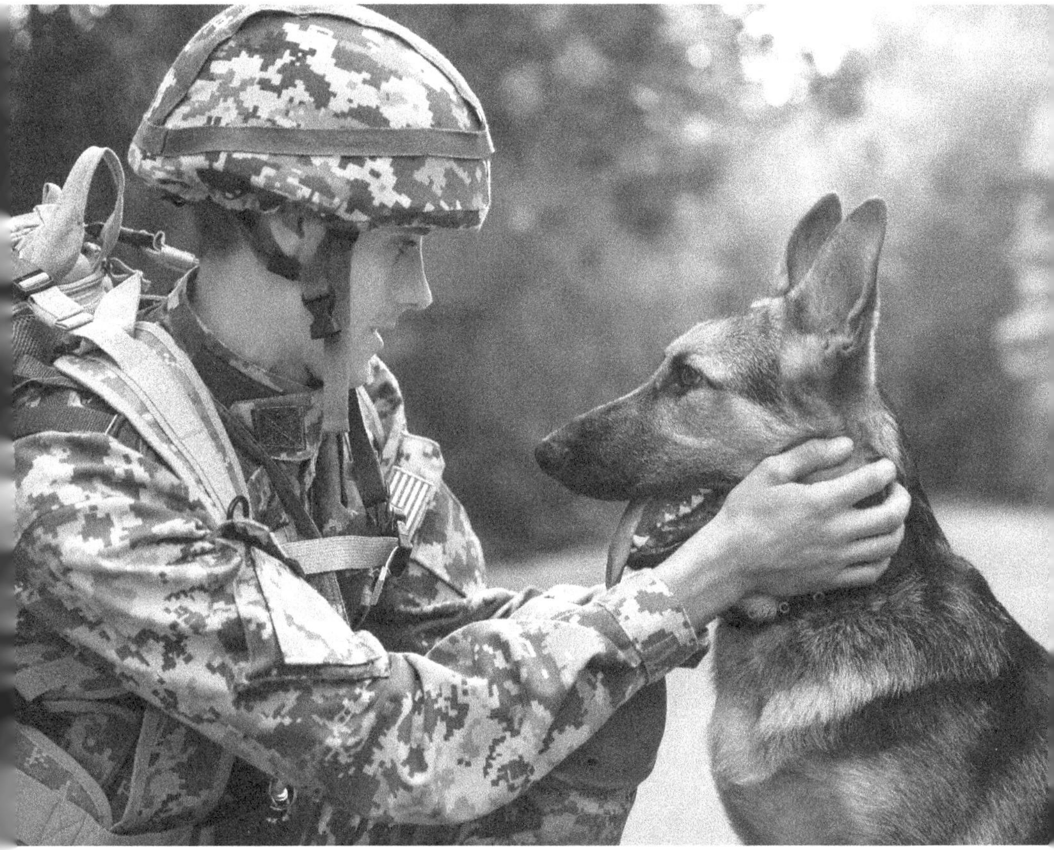

BAD TIMES, BAD TIMES

I've got a lot to remember about Vietnam and hardly any of it was good, even though I sometimes say it was "good times, bad times." The good times were making friends and changing as a person.

How I changed was bad and still is because of the Post-Traumatic Syndrome I got there. It's because of the way I slept on the floor when I got home, and Mom had to turn the TV and the phone down, so you couldn't hear it.

There were other bad things other than PTSD. How about being in the rain for 16 straight days, being "in country" for 14 months, and more firefights than I can count, sitting in the clouds of Agent Orange, and losing six close friends.

When I was growing up or going to school or even after, there was no way that I could imagine that my life would turn out to be controlled by a war thousands of miles away. But that's what happened. I was 22 years old and working for the City of Philadelphia Gang Control, where we certainly had our hands full, there being so many gangs and so much gang activity like mob fights, shootings and so on. And I was getting over a busted knee and along comes this letter telling me I've been drafted.

I was an only child, my dad worked construction and my mom made jewelry. My stepfather was in the Korean War. I grew up near 12th and Oxford and it was a good, nice life. I remember playing with my friends and the sound of the ice wagon coming down the way. We had the first TV on the block and wasn't that something.

School was fine. I played basketball and was on the fencing team also and had an after-school job at Lit Brothers Department store. There was gang stuff going on, but I was all right. In fact, the only trouble I got into involved those lions. There were two big stone lions in front of the school and the tradition, the rule was when you started at Edison, you were supposed to kiss their backsides. I absolutely refused. "I'm not kissing no lion's ass," I insisted. And that was that.

Then the next thing I know, I'm on the 8th floor at 401 N. Broad Street and there was a big sign, "Welcome to the Army." I went by bus from there to Fort Dix in Jersey. There were three other Philly guys with me, and I did okay because I was 22 years old, which made me for sure, more grown-up, and able to handle myself. I also pushed harder at basic training. I could handle it and was in the best shape of my life after basic.

I went on to Fort Sill, Oklahoma, which is less than a hundred miles from Oklahoma City. There's a lot of history there which goes back to the old west. In fact, the famous Apache, Geronimo, died and is buried there. They say that's where the cry of "Geronimo" when jumping out of a plane comes from.

I got trained up in artillery and communications in my eight weeks at Fort Sill. Then I heard about jump school which was at Fort Campbell, and I volunteered to become a paratrooper.

I really liked that, and the uniform and jump boots were cool, although my first jump was scary. Before long, I got my orders for Vietnam and started there as an E-4 at Cam Ranh Bay, which was used by the Army, Navy, Marine Corps, and Air Force.

Camp Eagle, also known as "LZ El Paso" or "LZ Tombstone," was my next destination. It was only about five miles from the DMZ. I was attached to a grunt unit and was the forward observer with my second lieutenant. I also was in contact with the artillery all the time, reading grid squares and using my "25," which was the almost-indestructible field radio. The only thing I could say was wrong with that piece of equipment was that the antenna made the radio and me easier targets.

I made sure to do everything I could to take care of myself, from following the instructions of "take care of my feet, my private parts and M16," to circling our position with mines to keep us from getting snuck up on. I also sent cassette tape letters to my mom and stepfather whenever I could.

Still, it was rough. I had so many near-misses, I couldn't count them. This had me eating plenty of dirt, trying to get as low as possible. And then there was the couple of real firefights I was in every month. Maybe the worst thing was being shot at and you don't know from where.

I didn't get away without paying a heavy price, which for me, was bad PTSD, which not only got me disciplined when I was still in, but had me treating for drug and alcohol problems when I was back to civilian life.

First thing I did when I got home, was surprise my mom. Not really the best idea because she fainted! Then after things calmed down for me, I got a job at Amtrak, then TastyKake, and after that, I worked for 25 years at the Budd Company.

I eventually got my 100% disability after chasing it at the VA for 33 years! The best thing is the family I made, including three grandchildren, which are all like miracles for me.

MESSED UP

I grew up in the Richard Allen projects, which if you're not from Philly, you don't know what they are, and you don't want to. The projects were high-rise buildings in the ghettos, originally built so the politicians could have more votes in a given area.

They were crime-ridden, dirty and dangerous, so bad that they had to have their own police force because the City cops wouldn't go in there. The maintenance of the buildings and the individual apartments were awful. There was crime all the time because of the drugs and the gangs, which included The Valley, Diamond Street, Oxford Street and more.

I lived there with my mom, two sisters, and my older brother, Dennis. Things were so messed up, I didn't even know for sure my right name, and when I went to the mostly white schools, I thought my name was, "Nigger."

After going to Ludlow Elementary and then Ferguson, I went to Penn Treaty, which was predominantly white. Then it was off to Thomas Edison in 1963.

The school was all boys, and I loved it, even though I got held back in the 11th grade and finished a year late. I was a long-jumper on the track team and almost won the City Championship. Football was my great love, but I had to pass on it because I couldn't buy myself the pair of cleats that I needed to play.

The section I was in at Edison was called, "The Trades Preparatory Program" where I took mechanical drawing. My teacher told me that I was so good that I should consider going to college. This got me really excited, but then he also told me something else. I should consider the Drexel Institute of Technology, because they didn't have too many negroes there. This raised my expectations, but at the same time crushed them.

There were no jobs to be had, so I went into the service, which a lot of guys did. At least for three years, you knew you were going to get paid which was the reason a lot of us went. Patriotism had nothing to do with it.

I went in the service on June 21, 1966. My mom went with me to the induction center at 401 N. Broad Street, and then I walked to the train at 30th Street Station. On the way, I was thinking about the fact that I was going out of town and also about the time that my friend, Ronnie, came back to Edison while he was on leave, and he was all decked out in his military gear.

I did my basic training at Fort Jackson, which was in Columbia, South Carolina. I never got homesick or anything like that and in fact, liked the physicality even though it was rough because it was in the middle of summer. Following orders didn't bother me either, but I did not like getting hollered at.

Before long, I was on track to be a paratrooper, which I knew I was going to make. That meant advanced training at Fort Gordon and what they called, Fort Crockett. The training was rough and some of the guys were crazy, but all and all, I liked it.

The next step was even harder and that was Jump School at Fort Benning, Georgia where they gave the airborne training. You had to be in great shape and pay attention all the time, but you also knew that you were special because you were training like The Seals, Rangers, and Marines.

Our first jump was up a spiral staircase and off a thirty-four-foot tower. I knew it was serious business, but I was all in. And the next thing I knew, I was jumping out of a plane and that was before I had flown anywhere in one.

This got me the "wings" we wore, which we called "our blood wings," and we got to wear the special blouse and the boots and the hat with the glider on it.

Next stop was Fort Campbell, Kentucky, and the 101st Airborne. I saw a neighbor from back home and Edison, George R. Martin. He was serving chow and while we were waiting to go to Nam, we had leave together in December of '67, which was right before the enemy's Tet offensive, which all of us soldiers knew we won, but the papers and TV and whatnot said the opposite.

We finally did go to Vietnam where we landed at Ben Hua. We stayed in the south doing proficiency training and then headed north where George and I were in the same company although different platoons, his ahead of mine, when we went out on a mission in Thua Thien on March 24, 1968. He was a machine gunner, and we had told everybody that we were cousins we were so close. "Street" or "play" cousins is what we called it back home.

Then I hear somebody call out, "Hey, they got George." He was just 18 when he got hit by the sniper, and they let me put a poncho on him and put him on the chopper. I went back to our base camp for a couple of days. I wrote his mother, Thelma, a letter, excerpts of which was published in *The Philadelphia Evening Bulletin*, which was the afternoon Philly paper back then.

Aaron Thomas was another guy from Edison that I knew, who got killed in Nam. He was on the Edison track team like me, but died in a firefight on November 4, 1966, in a place called Tay Ninh.

By the grace of God, I was never hit even though I was in a lot of combat. There was a lot of killing. A lot of dying. I was very afraid at first, but I did what I had to do even though I often said to myself, "What am I doing over here?" or to my buddies in the jungle, "I'll be glad to get home. I miss the concrete."

Altogether I was out in the bush for 11 ½ months, which was 2 weeks before getting out. I never even got out of that country for R and R. And when I "was short," or close to getting out I got nervous that something was going to happen because I was so close to going home.

I remember when I was on the plane to the U.S., I just couldn't believe it and even though we landed in Oakland, I don't remember anything except the stares and jeers while I tried to eat a steak dinner in my uniform.

Then we stopped over in Chicago and I'm facing 150 Hell's Angels while I was taking in the sights. But nothing happened, and I got my flight to home where I got to stay for 30 days before I had to go back to Fort Bragg to finish what little time I still owed.

My mom was in the hospital when I came home, and she just couldn't believe it when she saw me. I guess that's because I didn't even give a thought about how she would feel when I was there.

Things were really bad for me for a long time and many things never did go away. I am blessed that my wonderful wife and I have been married for more than 35 years. I got my Bachelor's Degree and was a drug and alcohol counselor and then a Probation Officer until 2013.

In between that and Vietnam, I had a breakdown and was in the hospital for that for a couple of months. I was given Thorazine for what they said was my explosive personality, which I didn't have before Vietnam. I was drinking and smoking weed heavily and then became addicted to heroin and was convicted for burglary.

So, my life has been very complicated. I am blessed with the peace of the present. The other part is something I must work to forget.

GHOST JOB

I came from a military family. My father was in the Army in World War II, as was my uncle. I was in the Boy Scouts and Civil Air Patrol before I enlisted in the Marine Corps. My two brothers who lived with me on the 2800 block of Marvine Street were in the service also. My older brother was in the U.S. Army in Korea and Europe, and my younger brother served in the Navy in the Mediterranean.

My best friend from Stetson Junior High until Edison, which he dropped out of, was Mark Smith. He was what you called, "Happy go lucky," and came from a family of nine kids. We had a great time playing stickball and so on until he was drafted in September of 1965. My best friend died in Vietnam on May 18, 1967.

When I enlisted in the Marines, the country was tearing itself apart over the War and those on my family's side of the argument were saying that the enemy was just laughing at us while we were having to fight a war with our hands tied. And, no way were we baby killers or anything like that.

I was always pretty responsible and had jobs at Albert Einstein Hospital dietary department and Strawbridge and Clothier department store in addition to Scouts and Civil Air Patrol and playing football in high school. So, I was confident when I discussed enlisting with my father. Like I figured, when I did ask him, he said that was my decision because I was "of age."

After I enlisted, I was sent to Fort Jackson which was in Columbia, South Carolina, and then I was sent to Fort Gordon. My AIT or Advanced Infantry Training was back at Fort Jackson where I was trained to be a truck driver.

The guys around me said it was a "ghost job," that it was easy, but I knew from my father about "The Red Ball Express" which he was in. Folks said it was a do-nothing job and it was all black truck drivers, but that was no way true. About the truck driving, it really didn't matter because soon I was in logistics as a supply clerk. Then I volunteered to be a paratrooper. I felt that if I was going to be in Vietnam, I wanted it to be in a unit that trained to fight, and I would jump into enemy territory where it was all about survival.

I was in the 173rd with George Bembischew and Del Younger and went to Fort Benning on a new adventure. I was ready to take on the world. When I was trained and ready for my qualifying, I double-checked all my equipment and then I was right next to the door and the next thing I know, I'm out into the sky because my sergeant said, "Go!" and I could see everybody else coming out. It was beautiful. Then, when we had all landed, we got into formation and marched over to the ceremony where we got our wings. It was very gratifying.

I didn't call home to tell my folks, but after, I got transferred to Fort Bragg, which was when I got my first leave. I came home for Mother's Day. I had all my airborne gear on. My dad said, "Your mother's going to have a fit!"

"Hi, Mom," I said when I went inside. "I'm home, and I'm a paratrooper!"

"What's that?" she said. "I didn't give birth to no fool!"

Besides that, all went well, even when I told them I was going into combat, which is what we all we did from Bragg, meaning to go to war in Vietnam. First, they flew us to Oakland, and then we were on ships for 21 days, stopping only at Manilla. About then, I was wondering whether I was in the Navy rather than the 3rd Battalion. This was especially true when we landed just as the 7th Platoon was coming then. It was October 1, 1967.

Paratrooper or not, I never put a parachute on my back during the nine months I was in the field. It was more like putting myself in a cesspool, which is what a rice paddy is, and us sitting in the dung of water buffalo sitting there for hours and sleeping in it.

I didn't actually remember the names of all the different firebases I was at, although many were near Pleiku or DakTo. We'd set them up, resupply and before long, we're breaking them down. There were lots of encounters with the enemy and none of them were "ghost jobs," except sometimes the way the enemy came on us or us on them. One engagement, I'll never forget.

We were to set up an ambush and I was to position a 50-caliber machine gun. However, I made the mistake of not bringing extra ammunition. We opened up on the enemy just fine, but before long, our base load was exhausted, and we were out of ammo.

As the NCO in charge, it was my fault and we had to pack up and retreat. Things could have gone bad for us, but we were lucky and made it back. I have lived with that and replayed it for more than 40 years, and it will probably last forever.

What I will never forget is how hard the last three months were. Those ninety days, we called it "short time," were the most terrifying of all the time I spent "in country," and nothing at all is like that fear I felt.

What also will stay with me forever is the camaraderie, the bonds I formed with the guys I served with, all the way back to Fort Jackson and Bragg. Like when I was the only person in the barracks and my old classmate, George, comes in and we both yell, "Edison!" It was the same way my buddies from the service, Rodney Janner, and Doug Billings, yelled "Airborne" when we met again, decades after the war.

My coming home when my tour was over was quiet, even though I might have been happy because I was able to get my discharge fifteen days early. The first thing is I'm back in the states and landing in Seattle. The next thing I know, I'm on the subway at Broad and Snyder.

I just wanted to get home to my parents. They had moved to Mt. Airy, and I remember walking down the street from the corner.

I had received news that my father was hurt on the job and had trouble standing and could hardly walk. My god sister was sitting there with her hand on him. But when he saw me, he stood straight up and faced me.

"Where's Mom?" I asked.

"She's in the kitchen singing, 'Near the Cross,'" he told me.

I could smell the cooking as I went to her.

"What's for dinner?" I asked.

And she started saying, "Thank you, Jesus, thank you, Jesus. My son is home. My son is home."

THIRTEEN CENTS

I enlisted in the military one week after I turned eighteen. It was because of President John F. Kennedy's speech about serving your country and what he had done. The school bus driver had it on a portable radio when I was thirteen, and I never forgot it.

My family and I grew up in North Philly. It was my dad who worked at an electrical company on Aramingo Avenue and mom, my sister, Ana, and my brother, Fred, and me.

I dropped out of Edison High and got a job at Daroff's which was a well-known manufacturer of men's clothes. I became a presser and a pretty good one because I got to work on special jobs like the suits for TV star, Dick Van Dyke.

What I was waiting for was when I turned eighteen because I still had that speech in my mind and the week after my birthday, I enlisted in the United States Navy because of John F. Kennedy's exploits on PT-109, which became a famous book and a movie starring Cliff Robertson. Lieutenant Kennedy earned a Navy Marine Corps Medal and Purple Heart for his bravery after his small patrol boat was rammed by the Japanese destroyer, Amagiri.

I enlisted in the Navy without telling my parents, which made them very angry. The next thing I know, I was on the train which I caught at the North Philly station and headed for my basic training at Great Lakes on June 17 or 18 of 1968.

I did all right at boot camp and then was sent to Treasure Island which was near San Francisco. I spent two months there awaiting my orders and in the meantime, I worked in a warehouse.

While that was going on, I saw people at their best and their worst. I became good friends with a small group of guys, including Ray Rivera, who was also from Puerto Rico. We had good times together on base and visiting San Diego and Tijuana. At the same time, there were all these civilians protesting the U.S. for being in the war, which made me angry because these people had everything anybody could want, except, of course, a clue what was really going on.

The next thing I knew, I was on a truck which was headed for Camp Pendleton, which did not make any sense to me because that was for Marines and not the Navy. While I was there, I had amphibious training with the USMC and the Seals, which I felt more comfortable with since I was in the US Navy. The training was hard, and we learned a lot about survival and counter-insurgency.

The thing I remember most was our drill instructor walking down the line and his asking us what we think our lives were worth, and we're thinking $16,000 you know, from the insurance. He said thirteen cents because that's what a bullet costs! I never forgot that because it meant in combat, my life was cheap and easy to lose.

I should also say that I only wrote home once and that was during my whole time in. Maybe it was because I was so busy and whatnot. More likely, it was because my mom was so angry that I went over to Kensington and Allegheny Avenues (K & A, we called it) and signed up for the service while my parents were at work and me not telling them first.

Then soon enough I got my orders, and I was off to Vietnam with a couple of dozen other guys. I was assigned to the 3rd Marines and wearing fatigues, although with a blue belt to signify my still being Navy. But I never thought that would happen. I thought I was going to be on a nice big ship, and here I was heading for the jungle.

Our plane landed in Da Nang. It was February and it was in the 80s with more humidity than you can imagine and the unforgettable smell from the barrels of burning excrement. We were near Highway 1, and within thirty miles of the DMZ. That's where this sailor was carrying his M16, .45, M60 and a grenade launcher.

After a while, I started getting used to it. That's to the extent that such a thing was possible, because not only were we in combat, but we took plenty of incoming mortar fire, which also meant that Charlie wasn't far away.

All in all, it could've been a lot worse. I got to come home with all my parts working except for the kidney cancer that the Agent Orange gave me. The idea was for the chemical to kill all the vegetation and take away the enemy's cover. We could feel it on us like it was raining. The main ingredient of that defoliant, stored in the 55-gallon drums with an orange stripe around it, was dioxin, which scientists said is the most poisonous chemical known.

The non-combat part of my service wasn't as bad as it could be. The races got along ok except when there was really heavy drinking. We did get R & R, which meant "Rest and Recuperation," or "Rest and Relaxation," or as we sometimes called it, "Rock 'n Roll."

Everybody was allowed to take it once during their tour of duty after you had completed your thirty days in country. You put in for it, including your preferred destination, and you'd get your assignment, which could mean a shorter or longer wait depending on how popular the destination you picked was. The destinations included Hawaii, Australia, Tokyo, Singapore, and others. Like I went to the Philippines. There also was in-country R&R, like at China Beach, but that only lasted a few days.

When you got your R&R assignment, you headed back to your base, got into your khakis and flew-out commercial. Where I went, you could find a girl with no trouble, and the place wasn't that expensive. It was like Bangkok, but not as wild.

The time in country went by slowly, and sometimes, just the opposite until one day you're "short" which is also called "short-time," which means only two more months to serve. Then I was back in "The World," and I had been awarded three Bronze Stars and a Gallantry Cross.

I went back to Daroff's to work for a couple of months, and then Somerset Knitting Mills and Good-lad. After that, I was in the lighting business for eight years. After more than twenty-five years of fighting for my Agent Orange benefits, I succeeded with the help of the Disabled American Veterans.

The trouble was caused by the fact that whenever I filed or applied or pushed ahead, the VA would tell me that no way I got cancer from the Agent Orange because my paperwork was clear that I was in the Navy.

I'm married and have four children. By far, they are the awards I'm most proud of!

SMILEY

I grew up on 20th Street in North Philly with my parents, a brother, and four sisters, one of whom served in the Navy. We moved to our house in 1959 and were the only black family in four square blocks. The rest were mostly Irish and Italians.

I remember people walking by on their way to Connie Mack Stadium, which used to be called Shibe Park. It was at 21st and Lehigh. I had never seen so many white people before.

We used to tell them that we'd watch their cars "for a quarter" or rent them parking spaces, which were both a hustle. But that's when I learned it worked both ways. Some little white kid, who was walking by with his father said, "Look, there's a chocolate man."

The guys from my neighborhood went to Edison, Ben Franklin High School and Central, which were all boys. What I liked about school was that I could play football, which I dreamed of doing because a neighbor of mine had played college football and became a police officer.

I loved the game and played offensive guard and linebacker. Special teams as well. Going every single minute in my leather helmet. So high school was good. It was my plan to play pro football, but I also really liked art and mechanical drawing.

Then things fell apart at home. My parents separated and then a couple of months after they got back together, my father passed. Then, my mom who was a private duty nurse began having health problems and we had to move back to D.C.

I went to Anacosta High School to get my credits so I could graduate. There were about 200 people who came out to football practice, but even though the team was already selected, I got the coach to give me a try-out and I outran everybody because of my great footspeed.

In three days, I had taken over middle linebacker! We played Dunbar next, and they had a guy who was going almost 200 yards a game. Everybody called me, "Smiley," because I never did. But singing was something else. I saw Jimmy Hendrix perform in 1964, which blew my mind, so I started singing Hendrix while I'm battering their star running back and holding him to four yards total.

Because of my football exploits, I got four recruiting letters from colleges: Missouri, Kansas State (where Wilt Chamberlain went), Kentucky and Iowa. However, I had to go back to Philly to take care of my mother, whose health had become a roller-coaster. At home, I worked for years at a fancy hotel on Broad Street in Center City because of my ability to read floor plans. The hotel became famous worldwide, but not for a good reason. Twenty-nine people died and almost 200 got very sick because of a disease that grew in the water system. Because there was an American Legion Convention there at the time, it was named, "Legionnaires Disease."

In the meantime, I had already made friends with the TV football sports analyst, James Brown, who they called "J.B." He was not only a television person for CBS, but had been a big-time basketball player at Harvard University. I also had a good relationship with Hall of Fame Pro Basketball player, Adrian Dantley, and Temple Football Hall of Famer, Skip Singletary, who played pro. He was the first Temple Football player to have his jersey retired. It was number 64!

All of this reignited my passion to play football, and I attended try-outs with the Miami Dolphins. I was still really strong and quick, although maybe not as much as before because of my time off. I got to suit up and was in camp for more than a month, and getting paid for what I loved most. Much to my disappointment, the story didn't have a fairytale ending, and my football career ended when I didn't make the roster.

I was depressed when I had to leave the Dolphins which brought me to enlist in the United States Navy. They sent me to boot camp in Orlando because there were some renovations being done at Great Lakes.

Things started well like they did with the football, but had the same kind of ending, more or less. I became a Master at Arms and then went to aviation electronics school. I was also training sailors to swim and playing basketball and football. Then I hurt my left knee. It was bad. I received a medical discharge, and my career in the United States Navy was over.

I was glad when I was back home, but at the same time, I wasn't. My friends Larry Bell and Henry Carter were in the Navy and we were glad to see one another, although Kenny had been transporting bodies in the service and couldn't get rid of the smell that was still with him.

On the other hand, I had three friends who were killed in Vietnam: Jake Swift, Adolfo Martinez, and Antonio Garcia. Lots of my other friends came home with PTSD, and I felt guilty that I was home and not in the jungle.

Then things got better, or at least more stable. I worked at Radnor High and then Bartram, where for almost fifteen years I did security and was known as the guy who walks the halls singing gospel.

I got married to a great woman and have two children, a son named after me, and a daughter. So, I guess you could say that the name "Smiley" was for a good reason after all.

TWENTY MORE YEARS

I grew up at 22nd and Master Street in North Philly, 2242 W. Harlan Street, to be exact. It was me, my older brother by two years, Charles, who we called, Poppy, and my great-grandparents. My mother died in 1955 of kidney disease because she couldn't get dialysis. My great-grandfather died from a beating.

I went to Elementary School at Reynolds which was at 23rd and Jefferson Street, then to Vaux. Jr. High and then to Edison for high school. Peter Jackson was my friend for all this time. The tradition at Edison was that you had to kiss the backside of one of the two stone lions when you came in as a freshman.

This so-called "tradition" was essentially universally followed and was enforced by the upperclassmen, particularly the athletes, and it was backed by the principal. So, this combination of tradition and enforcement almost universally followed. I say "almost" because yours truly wouldn't be taken-in or bullied.

In any case, Edison was a great time for me. I became an amazing dancer and was known by my new nickname which was "Heatwave." I had my friends, ran cross-country to get my varsity letter, and had a good part-time job at the Morris Market which was in the 2500 block of Columbia Avenue. I worked there as a schoolboy until 7 at night on Tuesday, Wednesday, Thursday, and Saturday.

Everything was doing fine until this draft for 18 and up occurred when I was living at 1510 N. 18th Street. There was this letter that said, "Greetings," and that I was drafted, but it went to 1501 N. 18th Street. I learned that Uncle Sam wanted me from my friend, Dickie Roach, who was laughing when he told me. I wasn't laughing because the mix-up with the mail meant that I only had three hours to get my stuff together and get downtown to Broad and Cherry. Anyway, I made it and told my great-grandmother goodbye as my brother, Poppy, was at Cheney State University.

So, I reported and had my physical when they discovered I had blood in my urine. I got an extension and got to go back home for a while until things cleared up, and then I went back and started my military service.

Me and a bunch of guys were sitting around, and this smooth gentleman comes in and says I need seven volunteers and I'm going to get them one way or another. Then me and my newly found friends all went to lunch. When we came back, 'Smooth,' tells us, "Welcome to the United States Marine Corps."

Next thing I knew, we were on a train from 30th Street Station to Paris Island, South Carolina. Our train arrives, and we're put on a bus which gets us in at two o'clock in the morning, when some Marine jumps aboard and yells, "Go, go, every living asshole. Get out and stand on the footprints." These footprints were waiting for us on the ground, and we did just as we were told.

We got processed, which included getting inoculated, having our hair buzz-cut, and receiving our equipment. By the time we hit our bunks, it was three AM. Two hours later was reveille and then a stick clanging a trash can in our barracks. One guy was still sleeping, but Sergeant Ramos woke him up by grabbing him and throwing him across the beds.

I weighed only 117 pounds at the time, and you would think it would be rough for me, but I loved the Marine Corps and found all the training to be fun, and if you were receptive, they trained you good and treated you fair. For instance, I didn't have any experience with guns, but I was able to qualify with both the M-14 and the .45.

After Boot Camp at Paris Island, I had my Infantry Training at Camp Lejeune. I also got fourteen days leave. It was 1968 and things at home were what I would call "sensitive" because of the gang and the anti-war sentiment about Vietnam. My family and friends, particularly the elders, told me to take care of myself, which made sense because even though dying never crossed my mind, there was no doubt that I was going to the War.

I took an eighteen-hour flight to Southeast Asia, which was bittersweet. I was excited but befuddled. I had an altogether different reaction when we landed in Okinawa. I was there for two weeks. There were lots of girls. I loved it. Vietnam was something else.

We landed in Da Nang and there were four things I would never forget, and none of them were good. First was the stench, which was barrels filled with burning shit and gasoline. Next was the heat, which you can't even describe as a feeling. It was so much more than that. You could actually see waves of it. Third was the smell of death. You knew what it was, and whether you could describe it, was something that you'd always remember.

Then there were our fellow marines leaving for home. You'd think they'd be glad as they left, but none of them were smiling. All their youth and innocence were gone, and the looks on their faces were, "I've been in this, and I'll never forget it. I feel sorry for you."

We were in combat almost before you could imagine it. We're issued our weapons and ammo and are off to base camp where we took mortar fire. Shrapnel got me in both legs.

I was taken back to Da Nang where I was hospitalized. When my wounds were healed enough, I was sent to work in the mess hall for a month. I had made friends with Staff Sergeant Young and Sergeant Avery and was living in a hooch instead of a tent.

Then because I had experience in bulk cooking, I got to work in the mess hall for another thirty days. I ran into Butch Thompson from Philly, and we're close friends even now. I also saw Billie Phau, who I worked with at Lady Bug and Villager back home. I remember seeing Billie carrying the flag in the close order drill marching. That's something I'll never forget.

I spent the rest of my tour in Nam. November 18, 1969, was my last day. We got no debriefing. They just brought us back and dropped us off. What I came home with was something I would never have imagined. There was no Purple Heart, but there was what I sometimes can call "a rich experience" and life-long friends.

There also was what the shrinks called survivor's guilt and addiction. I was severely addicted to grass and cocaine. My great-grandmother who raised me had died. My brother was in a wheelchair. And I was a dope fiend.

But the Lord was there for me thanks to Pastor James S. Hall, Jr., and I got some help at the VA. Now after 20 years of being an addict, I came to recovery and God. I am a deacon at my church and run a drug and alcohol ministry.

E and E

There were eight of us kids and we were raised with morality and to have morals. My father was a very wise man and worked hard at Allenwood Steel to take care of us.

My brother, Johnnie Lee, studied psychology in Paris. So how I managed to grow up loving adventure and wanting to go to Nam is something I don't quite understand. But that's the way it was.

Maybe it was the way I was raised combined with my experience in junior high which meant fighting to and from school. Warring with "The Morocco's" would certainly leave an impression on anybody. And there was the excitement of the sword fighting on the fencing team at Edison High where I went next, and we won the State Championship in 1963.

In any case, after taking some commercial art courses following graduation from Edison, I told my parents that I wanted to enlist. They were not happy about it, but I was eighteen so off I went to get inducted and to Fort Bragg.

At Bragg, I learned quick enough that there was another way that you could get taught how to do things. The drill instructor was waiting for us when we got off the bus. "You got 3 seconds to get in line," he told us. "And I don't care if you're white as snow or black as tar, from here on, I'm your mother and your father."

My time there was okay. There were five guys in my platoon from Philly which makes you feel like you're not by yourself which is a big deal in the beginning. Also, we had nice April weather, and the food was good.

Next was AIT at Fort Gordon, which was combat training. It was two months of tactics, fighting and weapons training. I liked that.

Then on to Fort Benning for leadership training and jump school. You had to run everywhere, and the DI's were worse than in basic and would kick your ass if they thought you needed it. Also, you better not get injured, because if you did, you had to start the training all over again. "Recycle," they called it. I did hurt my ankle, but I just kept my mouth shut and toughed it out.

There were two months in the NCO or Non-Commissioned Officer Academy at Fort Benning. The same barracks and chow, but we had our paratrooper wings from finishing jump school. We were not supposed to wear them, but we sure did.

We got two weeks leave which I used to go home. Then before I knew it, I was back at it. My dad drove me to the airport where he kissed me goodbye, which was the first time he ever did that. I supposed he was a lot more scared for me than I was.

My next stop was at Fort Lewis, Washington where the place was so overcrowded with guys on their way to Vietnam that many of us were sent to hotels or motels like the Sheraton or the Holiday Inn. From there, we boarded a plane that stopped at Alaska, Japan and lastly, we were there. I'll never forget when they opened the airplane doors at Cam Ranh Bay. That heat hit us like a ton of bricks.

My orders had been changed so that I was now in the 173 Airborne instead of the 101st. I was a "Spec-4" now and on my way to a week of "in-country" training.

Shortly after that, I came under fire for the first time. Unfortunately, it was from our own tanks. Fortunately for me and us, nobody was hurt.

What I needed after that was a good stiff drink, which was something I never had before because I was always careful not to get into trouble. For instance, I always walked down the middle of the street in Nam, because if you were close to a bar, the girls would come out, take your hat, and then run back inside. You had to go into the place to get your hat back because if the MPs saw you without it, you got "arrested," and there was discipline waiting for you.

I did get drunk for the first time in Vietnam, though. I ran into my uncle, Billie Brown, who was a cook and made this powerful punch with pure alcohol.

It was appropriate that they were calling me "Stoney" then because I was drunk enough to get into a fight with a bunch of ARVNs (South Vietnamese soldiers). We were rewarded by having to be in formation at 3:00 o'clock the next morning.

Of course, there was serious stuff, deadly stuff that you'd never forget. Even though I was a paratrooper, I was partnered with Linwood Gough, who was a corporal and a machine gunner. We got along good because he was from Philly like me.

We were guarding a checkpoint at a bridge after coming back from the boonies. Then we decided to go over to the Fire Support Base 274 to get a hot meal. Then the enemy started in with mortars. One of the rounds landed between me and Linwood. I was knocked down by the concussion, but my buddy got hit by a piece of shrapnel. I popped some smoke and a medivac came and got Linwood while I made it to a bunker. Corporal Linwood Gough of South Philadelphia was killed by that attack. If he hadn't listened to me about going for that chow, he'd probably still be alive.

That event changed me forever. It taught me not to make friends over there, and I did "E and E" or "Escape and Evasion" wherever I went and whatever I did. Also, the fact that I never got hit made me feel bad, not good. I never even had a scratch, even though I had bullets come so close to me that I could feel them go by my ear.

I guess because of my feeling guilty about all that, I joined the LURPS, which is "Long-Range Reconnaissance Patrol." We were a small, heavily armed group that went deep into the bad guy's territory. We would watch the enemy go by us with none of our people anywhere around. That was lonely and dangerous work, maybe what I needed. Certainly, what I wanted.

Soon enough, maybe, too soon, I was home. I remember coming into Philadelphia Airport. People were calling me "baby killer." All I ever did was what I was sent to do, and that no way was killing babies. And I had to do what I was ordered to do, more often than not with one hand tied behind my back. Even still, we won every battle which makes it crazy that people say we "lost" the War.

Even after I was home a long, long time, I was jumping from grenades that weren't there. I also brought with me prostate cancer and diabetes that I got from the Agent Orange mist that we used to sit in. Also, I was hospitalized twice for worms. One time, I was not allowed to eat anything solid, but couldn't resist some fried chicken and sweet potato pie for which I paid quite a price.

So, there I was and sometimes still am, feeling like I don't fit in anywhere and having nightmares. What kept me okay was going into the National Guard from 1975 to 2007, and the understanding of my wife which I guess somehow were my E and E all over again.

POETRY

My mom went back to school at age 77 and got all A's in psychology. My grandmom won a scholarship, but she couldn't go to school with it because she died, which was on Pearl Harbor Day. Maybe there's some poetry in that.

I write poetry under a pseudonym, "Rondu Lateek." One of my favorites is "The Wisdom Tree." Vietnam was the major part of my life, and it is certainly in my writing.

Before I went in, was okay, because my mom was "something." She worked at a place called "All Aluminum" and she sold insurance, which she was very successful at, second on the east coast. It was me and my mother and my brother, Vincent, who became a helicopter gunner in Nam. We lived in North Philadelphia on a street with a name straight out of poetry, "Monument Street."

I went to Carver and Vaux before Edison where I was in the class of '65 in Distributive Education. I also had a part-time job. Then it was the service.

I did my basic at Fort Bragg where they got me in shape. It was pretty tough. Then it was Advanced Training at Fort Polk, Louisiana. We were trained in tactics like "Escape and Evasion," where you had to get to a highway by 10 PM without getting captured. After only a twenty-yard head start, one of our guys, whose name was Hall, ran into a tree and knocked himself out.

The training got us ready for combat. There was great camaraderie, and we all were feeling kind of cocky but still, every one of us counted the days. And then we were there, landing in Cam Rahn Bay at night.

In combat, you didn't even have time to be scared. The Viet Cong and the North Vietnamese were like ghosts, you only saw their bullets coming.

I remember March 21, 1969, like it was yesterday, which I'm glad it wasn't. We were called into one of our bases that had been under siege for days. When we pulled in, we saw a 20-vehicle caravan which was blocks long. The enemy had jumped out of bamboo-covered holes. All the vehicles were destroyed and everybody killed.

I was on a mechanized personnel carrier and we had tanks and our artillery. The ground was flat and there was a mountain above us. As we were pulling in, I saw Lester from my neighborhood back home pulling out.

Then things got really rough. That night, three of us from my squad were sent outside of the perimeter of our base camp. There was a bunker on the other side of the barbed wire, and we were to set up an LP or listening post.

Then suddenly, the enemy is shooting, and their bullets were so close I could feel them. Our guys were shooting back at them. One of ours got hit, and I made it to the radio, which was covered in blood.

By now we're there for four hours of bombs and bullets and then there's artillery coming at us. We started low-crawling back and into our hooch where we hear our people saying, "We thought you were dead."

Then I heard about one of our squads being overrun, and I did that run like Jim Brown from *The Dirty Dozen* and got to the command post, and I'm screaming, I got to go get help. My sergeant tells me that, "we got this."

We went on patrol to get the enemy. It was the first time I actually saw them. We had gone out on an APC and up this steep hill with our M-79 and 50 cal.

We were told to dismount, which is when I had my first encounter with booby traps as two of our guys got wounded. Then I see a rocket launcher pointed right at us. My buddy, Al, takes it out, but when we hit another booby trap, we went back to base where we faced mortars and artillery for over a week.

There were other times like this. One time I'm on an armored personnel carrier and a rocket is coming right at us. We escaped and then made like John Wayne. Another time, we're in a small party and outnumbered. We're running through the woods and it's getting dark. Our lieutenant tells us we're not going to outrun them, so we got behind some boulders and covered ourselves with leaves, but it starts to rain, and I'm essentially by myself. Then the artillery comes in, and it goes on all night.

I got through that obviously, but there was always something. We did "short-range patrol" or "Slurp," which I hated. You'd be out four days and three nights and as often as not, you'd run into the enemy. Sometimes it was crazier than you could even imagine even when you thought you were okay.

One time my friend, Tommy, and I are set up in camp, and he got his 50-caliber machine gun readied, and it's black as night can be, except for this moonlight which shines on a giant tiger coming right at us. I'm ready to really light it up when Tommy puts his foot in front of the 50 Cal, which is telling me to back-off, so we didn't give ourselves away.

Being "short" meant you were nearing the time to go back to "the world." Usually, that was two months or so. Some guys would start marking off the time they had left on a calendar or a stick. But everybody who wasn't halfway crazy started taking extra care.

I was sitting on a truck parked on the edge of a cliff when I was short, like three weeks left. A flatbed swerved and lost control and boxes of ammo came down on me. My knee got it pretty bad, so they couldn't stitch it up. And I got sent to Camp Enari to recuperate.

Well, I was there getting better and closer to home when my buddy, Tommy, comes to me. He's begging me to go back with him, that they need someone because all the guys with him now are green. But I remember this guy named Parker, who was on his last day, with his wife waiting for him in Hawaii, and he goes out and gets himself dead.

So, I tell Tommy, no, and then I'm called back to the rear and my squad was out in the boonies with the ARVN whose war it's supposed to really be. Anyway, they run off and a satchel charge blows up my squad leader, and Tommy's really disfigured.

I got flown to Fort Lewis in Seattle where I kissed the ground and then to Fort Dix where I'm in line to set my signatures and so on to be discharged. My papers weren't the way they were supposed to be, but I got what I needed, and I was done.

I threw away everything I had that was green, but it was still no party. I went over as a boy and came back a man, but a man who had lived with the red ants and leeches and had seen death and dying. I had become a jungle cowboy who would not forget how inhumane people could be.

I got married to my Denise, and it's been 46 years and I worked for Philco Credit Union and for Acme for more than a quarter of a century. The VA says I'm 70% disabled, but it's more like I wrote in my poem, "War." "The wounds and scars can't be erased. The life that's lost can't be replaced."

THREE GOLDEN RULES

I'm pretty sure that my family life and what happened when I was young got me safely through the War that unknown to me, was waiting for me up ahead.

It was me and my two brothers and my parents living on Darien Street. We had two bedrooms and a cellar which had a coal furnace. I was an early riser so even when I was young, I had to shovel coal.

I was 5 ½ years old when my dad moved out and left us. That wasn't easy to deal with, but not as difficult as when I was 20 and my mother died because of high blood pressure. Fortunately for me and the other two kids, Bill and Jim, our father came back so we could have a life.

The service helped us have a life also. We had a tradition of going into the armed forces in our family. My Uncle Joe joined in 1939 but never spoke about his experiences. Uncle Jerry was in World War II also, but unfortunately, he was shot in the neck.

While I was never told for sure, I think it was the idea that our family served that played a big role in my brothers going in and then me following. My brother, Bill, served four years in the United States Navy after the Korean War. Jim was in Okinawa but also was in Vietnam for a short time.

It was Jim who was my mentor. He gave me the three rules of growing up:
    a. Always ask out the pretty girl.
    b. Never get sucker-punched.
    c. Never go down in a fight.

It was also Jim who took me to the draft board at 401 N. Broad Street when my time came.

I started my education at Fairhill Elementary at 6th and Somerset. Later on, I went to Saint Bonaventure and then to Cardinal

Dougherty for a while. Along the way, someone badly mistreated me which made me somebody who hated bullies afterward. It is also how I got thrown out of school and into Edison High School.

Edison was 1,500 guys, and I had a good time even though they put me in the general curriculum because I was expelled before. I had a great teacher, my favorite, Mr. Jaffee, who was a World War II tank commander and was not afraid of anyone.

I did well at Edison because I asked to be transferred into academic classes. I graduated with distinction, played football, and tutored math along the way. I also worked with my dad who was a painter and paperhanger.

After graduation, I studied two years at The Electronic Training Center. One night I was watching the news when I saw Henry Kissinger talking about peace, but the enemy walked away. Then I saw the demonstrations at the University of California, Berkley. I knew that the only right way was to win the fight. I enlisted on June 26, 1968, which got me active duty on November 1.

My experience serving my country was like my life, filled with bad stuff and good. For instance, when I was at Paris Island, I got in trouble for laughing which happened more than once. That got me doing a lot of squat thrusts.

I also did whatever I was asked to and qualified in everything. I also got punched by my drill instructor and broke my heel. All in all, I did good enough to move on to Advanced Training at Camp Lejeune. Like everything else, it was valuable hard work and what you would have to call, crazy. For instance, I handled all the arduous physical training, and I literally bumped into a bear.

After a month at Lejeune, I got to go home. My dad was nervous that what was next, was that I would find myself being a "bullet stopper." But fortunately for me, that didn't happen.

I was listed as a radio relay tech, which got me to San Diego, where I took some accelerated courses. We finished 15-week courses in 9 or 10 weeks. Then my captain asked me to do some teaching, which I did for another month.

Then it was time for Vietnam. I landed at Da Nang, where they didn't have any need for radio technicians. And there I was, in two firefights, which was scary. Then I was sent to Laos for four months which was tough.

Next, I was sent to Hue for five months which was much better. I played whiffle ball with the kids during the five months I was there, and the only injury I had was a minor one I got playing basketball.

After another month at home, I was sent back to Camp Lejeune where I got orders to be where they taught me about mines and ground radar. Then it was off to Quantico.

My time there seemed crazy, like everything else. But like everything else in my life, there was always something bad. Being in combat like I was, is terrible, so part of my life is like losing a family member every day.

I was home for good on the same day I enlisted. My dad had a party for me at our home. Then I worked at Girard College which was a school for fatherless boys. After that, I worked in finance for seventeen years and then sold life insurance. My working career ended with me being a tax agent for the state to which I could add my service time to my pension.

I was in pretty good shape and was running marathons. This enabled me to break up an attempted rape and catch the perpetrator who served seven years in jail.

So, what about the first thing, my brother James told me, the one about the prettiest girl?

I met my wife on the "el" which is the elevated local train in Philly. She was the prettiest girl I ever saw. So, I ran over and sat next to her. And just like it should be, we got happily married afterward!

ROCKET CITY

I grew up across the street from Connie Mack Stadium, which was where the Philadelphia Phillies and at one time, The Philadelphia A's or Athletics played their baseball games. Me and my younger brother used to be able to watch parts of the games through our window. We also used to tell the white folks who wanted to park their cars in our neighborhood that we would watch them so they didn't get broken into, but that was just a scam.

My dad had a good job at Progress Lighting where my uncle was a supervisor. Both had been in a war, my father in World War II and my uncle in Korea, but neither one of them would ever talk about it.

My growing up was pretty good because my dad had a good job, and my mom worked hard at her job. And there was my brother and the kids in the neighborhood. Every summer, I went to my grandma's in Maryland, which sounds like it would be a vacation, but it wasn't.

Me and my cousins called the 'so-called vacation' "*Stalag 17*" after the movie, or "Prison Camp." Grandma sent all of us to her cousins where we worked in the field. Without shoes. It was really rough. We got paid, although not much, and then we had to pay room and board. Our so-called cousin told us that if we complained, we'd get sent to a boy's home, which we knew was like a reform school.

Things were okay when I got back to school because working in the fields toughened me up. This was a good thing because I was basically shy, even though I acted like a playboy. I was also very lucky to have three close friends and was busy having a paper route and working at the corner deli. I also ran distance for the track team at Edison and played soccer.

With all of this going on, I never talked about the service, so my parents didn't believe me when I told them I was enlisting. In fact, my mom actually drove me to 401 N. Broad because she didn't believe I was going to enlist, which I very much was.

Next thing I knew, I was on a bus headed for Fort Dix which fortunately was nearby in New Jersey. The thing that stood out was that I met a guy named Frank Hatcher who was from New Jersey. Everybody was always mixing us up, and we even both went on to AIT or Advanced Infantry Training together.

Our AIT was at Fort Knox, which was in Kentucky, about twenty-five miles from Louisville. Fort Knox was named after George Washington's first Secretary of War and covered more than 100,000 acres. The temperature there went from below zero in the winter to over 100° in the summer.

While I went into the service as a wireman, I became a mechanic which had me road-testing vehicles for the Army, which I really liked. After a year at Fort Knox, I was given a choice of going to Okinawa or Germany. I was sent to Vietnam and then tried unsuccessfully to get out of the Army like in *Saving Private Ryan* because my cousin was in, but that didn't work.

I received two things in Saigon. First was my orientation and the next was two sleepless weeks. Then I was sent to Long Binh for a month. It was the center for nine major support commands and "LBJ Ranch" or just "LBJ," which stood for Long Binh Jail, which I fortunately never stayed at.

Next, I was off to Da Nang, which had been home for the Japanese and French before our marines landed on March 8, 1965, which is supposed to be when our first ground troops got involved. There was a big port and Airforce base, and China Beach, which was really My Khe Beach, which was a place to get your R and R. And I would say, add another "R" for "rockets" of which there was so many incoming, we called it "Rocket City."

When Rocket City wasn't raining down rockets, the place was pretty cool like there was no saluting the officers, and I met a sergeant major from Brooklyn and a captain who treated me pretty good and kind of took me under their wings. I also started working out with Tae Kwon Do which I really liked.

But when the rockets were coming in at us, it was a pretty different thing. For instance, once I was in the shower when we got it with a rocket attack. After that, I only washed up outside, using my helmet. Also, even though I was a mechanic, I did get into a skirmish with a VC and broke my wrist. Of course, I never got a Purple Heart or anything like that because somehow my medical records got lost or messed up.

May of 1974 brought me to Fort Bliss and San Diego, the place I left the U.S. from. I came home in my fatigues. There was no party and no parade. But my mom was sure glad to see me, and that was okay because I was good at saving my money, and I did a lot of partying. Even so, things were really rough on the whole.

I have PTSD, and the first few years back, I was afraid of hurting somebody. My wife Yvonne passed away, and my oldest son died in 1998. The VA gave me a hard time and still does, like when they told me I didn't have jungle rot on my feet without me taking my shoes off.

Some good things happened also. One Christmas Day, I remarried, and my wife and I say we were each other's Christmas presents forever. Also, I see some of my friends from the service now and then, and I worked 24 years at Progress Lighting where my dad spent his working life.

MY LEGS

I grew up at 13th and Poplar, in a row house with my grandmother. We lived in an apartment on the right side of the second floor.

It's funny what you remember about your life growing up; like my grandmom used "Sr." at the end of her name, and we used to put the trash out on the roof until pickup day, but once the reflection of the sunset lit all on fire. I went to Hartranft Elementary School and used to run home for lunch. Robert Crudup was my buddy, and we played stickball and box ball for hours.

When I got older, I went to Stanton at Broad and Allegheny, and I was appointed captain of the Safety Patrol. I learned a lot from that, and it was very important to me. For instance, your friends wanted you to give them a break, and the guys on the Safety Patrol wanted favors from me and resented my being captain. But I took the job seriously because it was easy to not do your job and one of the kids get hit by a car.

I had good opportunities in junior high, and I took advantage of them. For instance, my first sports were swimming and gymnastics. I could do a standing flip and iron cross and was on television doing exhibitions on the *Sally Starr* and *Chief Halftown* shows.

In addition to sports, I did good with the books. My favorite subject was math, and I also liked working. For instance, I made my own wagon and went to the market to help people take their groceries home. But my best job was working with the ice delivery man, who by the time he got to the third floor, needed some help. I'd get one dollar, and then off I was to the Jack and Jill for their day-old ice cream.

Senior high was at Edison, and it didn't start so well. There were two stone lions outside of the school. You had to kiss the lions' behinds. All the seniors were there and our principal, Dr. Clarke, supported the tradition.

I stayed active at Edison, playing football, track (I still hold the broad jump record since 1963). I also ran the 440 and 880 relays and hurdles and fenced and swam.

After graduating Edison, "politics" prevented me from getting a football scholarship, so I went to a technical school called R.E.T.S. in Upper Darby, where I took electronics. Then just like that, I found myself in the Marine Corps.

I had a friend who worked at the draft board, and he gave me a "heads up" that I had a letter coming. I wanted to do recon for the Navy, but my buddy, Eugene, and I wanted to go in by "the buddy system."

Then the way things turned again, it's just me and I'm heading for the Corps and basic training at Paris Island where the greatest bothers were the mosquitoes in July and M.Sgt. Land and Sergeant Burgoyne. But I learned to tolerate it all.

After Paris Island, I went to South Carolina for three weeks of Advanced Infantry Training. I was there when Dr. King was shot.

Then I was off to Camp Pendleton for mountain training. There were huge spiders and lots of snakes. After that, it was Okinawa for our inoculations. Everybody was sick from those shots.

My leapfrogging continued, and the next place I stopped was Alaska where it was plenty cold outside. Japan was next, but we weren't allowed to go anywhere. The next thing I know is we're in Da Nang, South Vietnam and I'm getting out of the plane and right into a firefight without a weapon.

When I joined Lima Company 3-7, my weapon was my best friend. When I first was given an M-14, it was literally filled with blood and guts and we had twenty-four hours to clean it perfectly which I did. I became so proficient that I could take that weapon apart and put it back together in the dark.

That M-14 served me well in lots of firefights, which was a good thing because my life depended on it. Even so, I also carried plenty of grenades.

Unfortunately, they replaced that fine weapon with the M-16, which was so fragile that it would break if you hit somebody over the head with it. And the parts were so small, if you had to take it apart or replace something, you could just as easily lose a part. It also wasn't very reliable. For instance, me and seven others were in an ambush and only two of us had weapons that worked. So we ran.

Like my M-14, Sergeant Stuckey kept me alive. He told us exactly what to do and told us that as long as he was there, we'd never lose a man. Then, one time he said that if he went on this mission, he wouldn't be coming back. Fortunately for the Sergeant, he had bad hemorrhoids, which because of some good luck and a smart corpsman, got him on a plane out of instead of in what he knew was his last battle.

When you're "short," it means your time to ship out for home is getting close, and you aren't supposed to do anything that could put yourself in harm's way. Everybody knows that.

Even so, the day before I was to leave for home, I volunteered to take a unit out. Everything went okay until we started back in. Then, I'm walking ahead of my men, and I step on a mine. It was 4:30 in the morning, there's no moon, and I'm flying through the air.

It was so dark, I couldn't see what had happened to my leg, which kept me from going into shock. Even so, I can still smell the explosion.

Then they tell me they can't get me out until daybreak because it's too dangerous to land the helicopter at night. We have a strong argument, and I let them know what's going to happen if they let me lay there.

Well, they came and got me. Even though my corpsman had no morphine left, I was okay because he gave me three very potent joints to smoke, and I didn't feel a thing.

Things got a little complicated when my helicopter landed in Da Nang. I had shrapnel in my groin and right near my heart, and this captain wanted to take both my legs off. Fortunately, a colonel overruled him.

When they sent me to the Philippines, I thought I was in heaven with pretty nurses, color TV and so on. Just as well, though, because otherwise was not so easy with me in a body cast from my legs up to my chest.

Then I was off to a naval hospital in New Jersey. I wound up having more than twenty operations and became a very nasty person, which got me into the psych ward more than once. "Shove your money. Give me back what is mine!"

Eventually, I progressed enough to get a job at the YMCA where I taught the kids about swimming and won a lot of trophies. I went to business school and worked at the Post Office and then for 30 years at Philadelphia Traffic Court.

I am married with five sons, and I compete in races. Unfortunately, they're in a wheelchair which I can talk about. In fact, I have to. If I don't keep letting it out, it eats me up. "Shove your pension," is the kind of thing I'd say. "Give me my legs back."

JUNE BUG

From the public housing projects with their gang wars to snow so deep it buried the cars in North Dakota, to the jungles of Vietnam, it seems like one movie or dream after another. But when it was all over, I knew that I had been blessed.

Public housing herded poor people, mostly black, to live in a compact area for political reasons, that is their votes. High rises were the most dangerous, but fortunately, my big family lived in a low-rise, not that the gangs like The Valley didn't want to put a beating on June Bug, who was me, whenever they got the opportunity.

So, things were rough, and we ate government surplus food, like those pieces of cheese, but neighbors took care of neighbors, and themselves, and family meant something, like going home from school for lunch when you were little.

High School was where it all happened. Where we didn't have much but were cool except when the gangs were after you. I had some good times there playing football and even being a class senator.

But on the other hand, it was the drugs and the gang wars and the fact that I couldn't get a real job. Chopping onions at 23rd and Diamond wasn't going to do it. Thank God, I chose the service instead of heroin which killed my friend, Tinker, or a shotgun blast from a member of The Valley Gang.

I picked the Air Force because of my best friends, Leon and Albert, were in. So, after my trip to 401 N. Broad and my two weeks of sitting home, nervous as could be, I was off to this new life. My stepfather told me when I left that the day I enlisted was when I became a man.

On June 22, 1965, I headed off to Lackland Air Force Base in San Antonio. It was so hot there that we had to wear sun helmets like they did on the television show, *Ramar of the Jungle*. One of the guys even died from the heat, but even still, we had to do what we had to do, what we were ordered to do, like march.

I don't know what prompted me to say anything to our drill instructor about it. But I did, even though I knew I was asking for trouble, which I almost got plenty of. When I said, "Sir, you march us like this in the winter?"

"You bet your brown ass, we do!" was his response.

So, we put up with the heat, even though at night you had to turn your bedding over two or three times. With all of us doing that, it was like a tornado.

Basic was tough, but I liked it. For instance, if your footlocker wasn't 100% neat, they dumped everything out. And there was all that marching, which turned out to be fun. We chanted, "GI beans and Gravy. Gee, I wish I joined the Navy." And we had another drill sergeant who had something wrong with his heel or leg. He called us all "girls," but he squeaked when he walked because of his injury.

After basic, I was off to Grand Forks, North Dakota, where it was as cold as it was hot before, and the snow was so deep, it buried the cars. The base was opened during the Cold War with Russia and there were big-time missiles there and the giant bombers of the Strategic Air Command.

What was most memorable was the brotherhood which I think was partly due to the weather. I met a guy named, Randy Stinson, from Pottstown, which we referred to as "Philly" because other places were so far away. We're still buddies, and my kids call him, "Uncle."

I was at Grand Forks for three years, 1965–1968, where I was a supply clerk and worked at the Base Military Exchange. It wasn't bad, and I got to travel like to Canada and learned to fish in the Red River in Minnesota. I also went to the University of North Dakota. Then I got my orders to go to Vietnam.

I had the same MOS, but I wasn't handling supplies in the good old USA, but in Cam Rahn Bay, where we had a big base where we handled lots of supplies and logistics. It was also a base for our F-4 Phantom II fighter-bombers.

I was also stationed in Nha Trang, which was originally an Air Force base built by the French and after we were there, was taken over by the enemy in 1975. But all my activities weren't limited to be on the base, and many times I was in the middle of things as we had to deliver supplies to downed airmen. Nha Trang was also one of the first places hit during the Tet offensive.

The War started to get to me, and even with my daily prayers and my grandmother, when I was discharged in Washington, D.C., I not only had the bamboo crossbow I had brought home but the Post-Traumatic Stress Syndrome that so many of my brothers had.

Fortunately for me, the treatment I got worked, and I was able to get my degree from Temple University and work for the Pennsylvania Human Relations Commission for more than a dozen years, first as a caseworker and then as a supervisor of 25 employees. So, I guess you could say my whole life was service. Not that I wasn't blessed for it from my mom who had a "Welcome Home" sign up for me and by my own family, which gave me wonderful children and grandchildren.

POW TO PARATROOPER

My family and I were Kalmyk, which is a branch of the Mongol people that moved to Russia. "Kalmyk," which means "remnant" is also called "Oirat." Our people were the only Buddhists in Europe.

I was born in Germany because my parents were captured by the Nazis and taken for slave labor. Also, my father was a captain in the Russian Army which was fighting the Germans. Needless to say, it was awful, particularly because a German soldier raped my mother. She had a baby from that, but it died. My father, who was a very honorable and caring man, saw to it that that child received a proper burial.

After we were freed by the Americans, we lived near Munich, which would have been around 1946. In 1952, we came to the United States, landing in New Jersey, and then moving to Philadelphia. We didn't speak any English, but we survived by many part-time jobs. My mom worked at Girard College, which is a boarding school founded originally for "orphan white boys." but which changed in 1968 to admit boys and girls of any race.

We lived at 1926 W. 3rd Street. It was a "working class" neighborhood. There were eight of us kids, of which I was the oldest. The four boys lived on the third floor. I remember that we ate lots of foods that we had in "the old country," like home-made bread and borscht which my mother prepared even though she was also working.

I started school at William McKinley Elementary School, which was so close by that I came home for lunch. Then I went on to Penn Treaty Junior High, which was pretty good because there were no racial fights or anything like that, but I stuttered a lot, so I had to take special classes. What I didn't have trouble with was sports, because I learned baseball and was a pretty good second baseman. I wanted to be like Granny Hamner, who played for the Phillies starting when he was only seventeen and went on to be an all-star, a captain and even play against the Yankees in the World Series.

From 1962 to 1965, I went to Edison High School. It was mixed race, which was all right with me because that's what I was myself.

We needed the money at home, so I didn't have much time for activities. I worked at a plywood company across the street with my brother, Dave. My pay was $1.25 per hour, which mostly went to my parents, although I was able to keep some which I put into the bank.

Of us seven kids, I was the only one who went into the service, which I did to pay back the United States of America which brought me here, the day after Christmas more than a dozen years before.

I remember when the Army recruiter came to Edison. We were all in the auditorium, and he was passing out cards about the service and joining. I told my brother, Dave, that I was thinking of joining.

The Vietnam War was just starting in June of 1965 when I went to the recruiting Center at Erie and Germantown Avenue and sat down with a black first sergeant and after listening to him, I enlisted, which they called "delayed enlisting" so I could work for the summer and what I made, I gave to my parents.

And then before I knew it, I was taking a train from 30th Street Station to Fort Jackson which was 50,000 acres big in Columbia, South Carolina. Most of the Army got their basic training there, which was called BCT, the "C" standing for "combat." It was named after President Andrew Jackson because he was born on the border of the Carolinas, and he was so tough in battle himself that he earned the nickname, "Old Hickory."

The motto of Fort Jackson was "Victory Starts Here," which I think it did for me. Even though the temperature could go as high as 90 degrees with lots of humidity, I felt good the moment I put on the uniform that I had finally found something in my life.

Then I shipped off to Fort Gordon, which was in Georgia. I got advanced training there and lots of army food, which was fine for me because we didn't have much to eat back home.

And then came the recruiter and asked if anybody wanted to volunteer to join the 82nd Airborne and become a paratrooper. So, I said yes, and there I was in Fort Benning, Georgia. I wasn't scared about jumping out of the plane because we had done some practicing from those high towers. Jumping out of a plane was the unknown which I quickly learned about. It was exciting! And in 1966, I got my paratrooper's wings pinned on me.

In April of the next year, I was a member of the Third Battalion of the 503rd Infantry as a paratrooper. We all knew we were going to go to Vietnam, but I was ready to go because that was my job. Soon we were off by ship which took us a month to get there, stopping in Guam and the Philippines.

I was assigned to the 173rd battalion and soon after, I was involved in my first combat operation. It was monsoon season and we went out on ambush patrols. It was cold and wet. And I was cold, wet, and scared.

This was around the time of the battle of Dak To, which went on for almost three weeks in November of 1967, against the North Vietnamese in the Central Highlands. The enemy had prepared for this for almost six months and the battle for Hill 875 was one of the bloodiest so that members of my Third Battalion and new paratroopers had to replace the Second Battalion. The result was that one-fifth of the 173rd was lost, 376 killed and almost fifteen hundred wounded. The enemy moved off to Laos and Cambodia. The 173rd Airborne Brigade was awarded the Presidential Unit Citation.

While I remained "in country" through the Tet offensive and went on patrol almost every other night, I don't think I actually came under direct enemy fire. I'm grateful of course, that in September of 1968, I returned to The World in one piece, while for instance, four guys in my squad were killed by booby traps on June 13, 1968. But at the same time, there is the awful feeling of guilt that everything went the way it did. I still have this with me of feeling guilty for leaving my guys behind, and me never getting hurt. And there's also the anger at the anti-war demonstrations when I came home. None of any of that ever went away.

On the other hand, Rosemary Brown was waiting for me when I came back. We wrote to each other daily when I was in the War and got married before the year was out after I got home. We were blessed with two sons, Steven and Kevin, and I also still have the memories of the closeness I shared with the men I served with like Bush and Reynolds.

After the War, I worked at Mayfair Lumber and then went back into the Army and was stationed in Germany and in Korea. Then I became an Airborne instructor. I served 22 years altogether and finished as a staff sergeant E6.

Then, I worked security for Spectraguard, and in my 40s, went to Temple University and earned my Bachelors of Science degree.

NIGHTMARE

I would never have guessed that I would be voted as "The Best Artist" in the Senior Class. Not ever. Not in a million years. After I was, I thought I would go to New York and be a painter, but that didn't happen. What I did was too awful to imagine, or forget.

Anyway, before that occurred, things were pretty good. My dad worked at Boeing Vertol (Vertical Take Off and Landing). They had thousands of employees and made helicopters. Their saying was "A Chinook a day," which was a helicopter.

He took public transportation to get to Boeing. It was called PTC back then instead of SEPTA. I think the tokens you needed to pay for the ride were 17 ½ cents or two for thirty-five. Even though he worked as much overtime as he could, my father still had time for me and my two sisters.

One of the things he did was tell me about World War II where he was a medic in North Africa. The Army was segregated, and it was pretty rough, he told me. He was very bitter about it all and in fact, told me that the two places you don't want to go are the Army and jail.

My mom was great, and when I came home for lunch from my elementary school, which was right across the way, she always had something good waiting for me. The girls did just what you would think, teasing me, but looking up to me at the same time.

My house was nice and so was my street, even though you could tell what they were cooking next door. Almost all my friends had two parents, although some was divorced. Tommy's father was killed in World War II, and the new kid across the street lived with his mother and aunt because his father was killed when he got hit by a trolley.

From the fourth grade on, and then at Gillespie Junior High, and then Edison, things were pretty good for me at school, too.

What with me getting to do art and one of my friends was with me. His name was Zeffro Gaskens, and he lives right across the street from me even now.

The one thing we all did have to watch out for, was the gang warring. The Avenue, Diamond Street, The Valley. "They didn't play," we used to say, and if you weren't careful, you could get beat really bad or shot with a zip gun, which was made from a car aerial but shot a real bullet.

I went to Thomas Edison High School and learned a lot about Thomas Edison because I wanted to be an artist, and he created over a thousand things, including the phonograph and light bulb. It turned out that he only went to school through the fourth grade and was deaf, but he had this really cool idea of getting in touch with his creativity. He held three ball bearings in his hand and underneath them was a big metal bowl so when he fell asleep, the metal balls would fall into the metal bowl and wake him up, and he would write down whatever he was thinking about in his sleep. I learned the worst lesson in my life later on, which was sometimes not knowing something while you were asleep could be the worst thing in the world.

My plan to go to New York City to become an artist didn't work out because while I was working at Sears after graduation to get enough money to follow my dream, I received a letter that started with, "Greetings." It was from Uncle Sam and meant I had been drafted. Both of my parents were really upset, but I couldn't do anything else except report to the Induction Center.

It was pretty scary at first, but at least I knew somebody there, Eugene Pace from Ben Franklin High. We went to basic training together then Advanced Training at Fort Bragg, which somebody told me was originally called Camp Bragg after some Confederate general. We were right near Fayetteville, North Carolina, and there were so many of us going to Vietnam, there must have been 50,000 of us grunts, also called "boonie rats," that they called the place, Fayette-Nam.

Where we went next, was for our AIT, at Fort Rock in Louisiana. There was a big sign there that said, "Birthplace of the Infantry Soldier," and another that said, "Fight, Win." No doubt this was the place that we would get our Advanced Infantry Training. It also wasn't called "Tigerland" for nothing.

The weather was like we would be living in, with the temperature near ninety and the humidity in the 80s. There was a place called "Tiger Ridge" where they had built a complete Vietnam village with booby traps, tunnels, punji pits and spider holes. The training was really hard, but our instructors made sure that we learned what we needed to and that we would be ready.

After that, I got to go home for almost three weeks before I got sent off from The World. Unfortunately, I was sick in bed for eight of those days. The rest of the time, I tried to party as much as I could without thinking of what was ahead.

Then it was off to the airport. My dad didn't go with us which was because of his old bitterness at the Army. My two sisters came along with Mom and my girlfriend, Penny, who I had met at a New Year's Eve party. Also, my buddy, Wendell, who later married Penny's sister.

The trip to the airport wasn't something you forgot. Neither was the flight from it. Oakland, Hawaii, Guam, Vietnam. When we finally landed, and the plane opened, you were stopped where you stood by the heat and the smell of burning crap.

The next thing I knew, I was headed to Pleiku, which was in Vietnam's central highlands and Qui Ninon, which was an important supply terminal. My ultimate destination then was Firebase 6, also called Hill 1001, which was set up during one of the bloody battles at Dak To.

I know I'll never forget that place. We were coming in on a helicopter and it was really my first day "in country." As we were coming in, our helicopter or "whirlybird" was taking fire, and we had to jump to the ground, right into the enemy's barrage.

I was all right, but after that, I spent six months in the jungle sleeping in foxholes as we went from place to place. What I wouldn't have given to sleep in a bed. It was really rough and dangerous, but I became good friends with Sam Patterson, who was from Elizabeth New Jersey, and John Lawler, who was a red-haired college professor from Vermont.

The next thing I know, I wake up in a hospital, and I'm staring at this blonde nurse, who I can picture even now. I didn't know where I was or why or how I got there, or how much time had passed.

Then I was told that I had a grand mal seizure, which I never had before and that I had been in the hospital for three days. During that time, my entire platoon was wiped out.

That was too awful to even think about, and I still didn't remember what had happened. My memory started to come back slowly, but the doctor had to tell me that I was in Vietnam. Then they sent me to Japan. Everything seemed like it was a hundred years ago. For some reason, my white blood count was high, and because of that and my seizure, I stayed in Japan for a month and then went to Korea, all the time dealing with what they had told me about my buddies.

I was put "on profile" because I was disabled from my head problems. This meant I didn't do much more than "police" or clean an area and guard the entry to my barracks.

This also meant I wasn't going to be sent back to Nam, which was good because it meant I was safe, but hard because while I was taking it easy, I couldn't do anything about what happened to my platoon or that so many of the guys I served with, got killed.

I have never gotten rid of all that guilt I felt when my buddies got killed while I was staying in bed. It is still with me all those years later. People call it PTSD, "Post-Traumatic Stress Disorder," but they just don't understand how bad it feels.

There was another thing that I know will be with me always. I was finally coming home and was in Grand Central Station in New York after landing at Kennedy Airport. I was in uniform and carrying two suitcases and my duffle bag. A little old lady came up to me and said, "Were you in the War?" When I told her I was, she said, "Can I kiss you?" Which she did.

To this day, I believe she was an angel sent by God to tell me I would be all right. And I guess I am, because I worked thirty-one years at Boeing afterwards and had two great kids. My daughter is a speech pathologist and a grandson is a school teacher. That terrible feeling of guilt is still with me, though, and I think it will always be.

"PETE"

I was born in 1947 and went to St. Malachi's elementary school. In the 1950s, we lived at 1713 N. Marshall Street, which is what they call North Philadelphia East now. Back then, we just called it "North Philly."

My parents got divorced, and my mother moved to 18th and Fairmount to open a "beauty shop," which was a hair-stylist place. I had two brothers, and we got along pretty well. Unfortunately, my brother, Johnny, died in a freak accident in which he had head injuries.

I liked school, okay, and there was a group of nine of us Latinos who all hung together. Myself, I'm from Puerto Rico. All of us went into the service. My friend, Victor Quinones, for instance, served in the Navy during the Vietnam War.

The day I heard President's Kennedy's famous speech about not asking what your country could do for you, but what you could do, I went and volunteered for the Navy, even though I was only seventeen. The recruiter made the effective date of my enlistment my eighteenth birthday. And when I turned eighteen, they called me. I did it not only because of JFK's speech, but so my brothers wouldn't have to go.

I went over to the Draft Board which was a huge building. They say it was the first skyscraper in Philadelphia. I got "processed," which meant I filled out a lot of papers and was given a pretty quick physical, which most everybody passed. Then they gave me a train ticket and forty dollars, and I was on my way.

I walked to the train station at 30th and Market and made the trip to the U.S. Naval Training Center at Great Lakes. I had never been on such a trip before or been on a ship, but I met a bunch of guys on the train who were going to the same place, so it was okay.

The first thing waiting for me was called "boot camp" or "basic." Also, "RTS" or "Recruit Training Orientation." There were older, more experienced guys there called "lifers" who guided us. It was a good way to become a grown-up.

Each of the eight weeks had a different name and a different purpose. For instance, there was "PT" or physical training, "weapons and drill," for instance, you heard the call for "battle stations," that meant everybody had a place to go and go there quick.

In about a month, I became RPOC which means "Recruit Petty Officer in Charge," which was because my company commander had faith in me. I was responsible for about 100 guys, which meant I was in charge of them, but also, I was responsible for what they did. A lot of them were from the South, and fortunately, they were all good guys.

Later we went to Newport News which was called "Harbor of a Thousand Ships" and was our largest naval station. That's where I got my nickname, "Pete," which I guess was more comfortable for my shipmates than calling me something Latino.

I worked my way to Storekeeper Third Class, also known as Third Class Petty Officer or SK3, on the USS Long Beach, which was a nuclear-powered cruiser commissioned in 1967, and was the first nuclear-powered surface warship in history. Our motto was, "Strike Hard, Strike Home." The Long Beach was made of steel and aluminum and powered by two nuclear reactors and traveled at a speed of twenty-five knots, which is about thirty miles per hour.

In our group was the USS Enterprise. It was nicknamed, "Big E." It was the world's first nuclear-powered aircraft carrier, and it was the longest naval vessel ever built. The third ship in our group was the Tarkington, and we were all in The Bay of Tonkin, sometimes referred to as the Gulf of Tonkin, where the War was supposed to have begun when it was reported that North Vietnamese patrol boats attacked the USS Maddox on August 2 or 4th.

Our ship was attacked by two Migs on May 23, 1968. Because of the speed involved, we had to act before the enemy was any closer. We engaged, and unfortunately, two of our crew were killed in action. However, we were armed with our Taos missiles which we fired, taking down the enemy when they were sixty-five miles away. This was the first surface to air kill in Vietnam and we were decorated with a Navy Unit Commendation. The following month, we repeated a similar action.

I spent three years and six months on the same ship, being out at sea for 45–60 days at a time. We had three decent meals a day and air conditioning, but at the same time, because we were an atomic ship, it felt like we were sitting on a nuclear bomb. Besides that, we were called to "general quarters" every single day and there was really no way to tell whether it was battle stations for real or just a drill.

On May 6, 1969, I completed my three tours, but I took something with me, which was the cancer I got from Agent Orange. It was true that I was on a ship, but as the storekeeper, I was responsible for delivering ammo, transformers, etc., which I did by going ashore, to pick up provisions. This is how I got exposed to the deadly chemical.

So, I got out and went home. I not only pursued careers in sales, including real estate, but I fought with the Veteran's Administration to get my benefits. Now I am fighting my cancer from the Agent Orange with beams of proton radiation, which I think is ironic because I spent all those years fighting for my country on an atomic ship.

BITTERSWEET

I went into the U.S. Army on November 9, 1967. I would say that and my whole life was what you would call "bittersweet," like my stepdad, who had been in the Army himself, coming with me when it was time to go and his slipping me $20 even though you weren't supposed to have any money on you. And him and me knowing that it was probably the best thing for me to go into the service because I was out running the streets and drinking like a fool.

Maybe the thing that said it all was me sending my allotment of $150.00 per month home so I could later buy my first new car, which was a 1969 Oldsmobile Cutlass. And quick as you could say anything, somebody stole it.

So, the Army and Vietnam were a big part of my life with all of its twists and turns, which is how my life has been. Two things stand out about the War, though. One is no way was I a "baby killer" or deserved to be called that. Second thing is that when me and my buddies get together at the Vietnam Center on Arch Street, the thing we do not talk about is war.

I grew up at 1754 Beechwood Street with my mom and stepfather. Now all the houses have been torn down and my street is gone.

I had a good time growing up even though I didn't have any brothers or sisters. I had lots of friends like Roland Winston, who was one of twelve kids, and now my best buddy. We had lots to do. There was shooting marbles, wall-ball, bean shooters, jacks and making home-made scooters. All as long as you were home by the time the street lights came on.

I went to Frederick Douglas Elementary School that I could walk to. School itself was okay except my teacher would whack you with a ruler and bang your head against the blackboard, which I'm not kidding about. Fortunately for me, my best friend, Roland, was in my class.

Junior High was at Vaux. It was a dangerous time then because of the gang wars that were going on between "DeMarco's," "24th and Rittner" and "28th and Oxford." What this meant was you went to school and came right home. You hung around and you were asking for trouble. Fortunately, I was able to avoid getting beat-up or worse.

Edison High School was next, and I liked it. First reason was my cousin, Wesley Jones, was there. Secondly, I got to play sports, and I was good at them. On the football team, I played both ways, guard on offense and linebacker on defense. I also ran track and was good at it: 45.3 in the quarter mile and 21 flat in the 220. I also did really well in the long jump.

After Edison, I went to Dobbins Tech for two years to learn about machine shop, working part-time at Wanamaker's department store. Dobbins sent me to work at a tool and dye company. I also worked part-time at the morgue at Temple University Hospital. Then Dobbins placed me at General Electric at 69th and Elmwood. I spent five months there before I went into the service.

My basic training was at Fort Bragg. It was rough, and they were always yelling at us, but I learned a lot of discipline from my sergeants who were a black and white team. There were a lot of physical challenges like the forty-yard crawl, and I wasn't a very good shot. Fortunately for me though, there were some Philly guys in our barracks, which made things easier.

My next stop was Fort Lee, Virginia where I went to quartermaster school for two months, and then in May of 1968, I was one of 300 on our way to Vietnam. Nobody said a word. We did get to stop in Japan, but that was only for four hours and they had guards on the doors. Also, the temperature was freezing, and we were in jungle fatigues.

We landed in Cam Ranh Bay where we stayed for two weeks, which was okay because they had a gym I could use. Then I was off to Chu Lai, which was further north. Most of the time there it was guard duty.

Then I went to Da Nang and went on convoys. My buddy, Krietz, who was from Chicago, got blown up.

I lived in a hooch with about a half-dozen other soldiers. They were good guys. We got hit by mortars every day about two o'clock in the morning. We'd all run down into the bunker. Then we'd go out on patrol.

You slept with your "clothes" on, which gave you jungle rot which was so bad I had to walk bow-legged. I still have a rash.

When my grandmother passed in 1969, I came home and stayed for twenty days. I also got R and R which I took in Thailand. Time went on and after six months "in country," you could apply for "early out," particularly after having to have my arm in a cast for six weeks.

I left for home on June 14, 1969, arriving at night, after being bumped off my flight in Denver. When I landed, I was in uniform and heard them calling me a "baby killer." But I was proud to have completed my service, and I went back to General Electric where I worked before I was drafted. I worked there for 32 years. But still, there are the memories that make me so nervous and the anxiety, so I can't sleep.

MY ESCAPE

I was born in Puerto Rico as one of 10 kids. My dad was a carpenter and a minister, and my mom ran the house, which you can imagine was quite a job. Two of my brothers were in the service, my older brother, Jose, who passed away, and Angel, who served in the Air Force.

We moved to North Philly when I was 3, and lived in a row house that had an extra story, which we really needed. Our house was heated by coal and it was the job of the kids to do the shoveling to keep the boiler going. Then we moved around a lot, renting different places like at 3rd and Berks, Diamond Street and Susquehanna.

Berks Street was where we lived the longest. Our neighbors were Irish and German, and there was one Russian family. Our house was close enough to come home for lunch, but I also remember having milk at school which was 25 cents per week. Growing-up was fun and we played in the street and made our own scooters. I remember though, you weren't supposed to sit on the steps, which folks took great pride in keeping clean.

After going to Penn Treaty Junior High when we moved again to Fishtown, we moved back again to our old neighborhood. I went to Edison High which I loved! It was the time of the Motown sound and I learned to socialize and play the guitar.

There were a lot of gangs around too, but my parents were very strict and religious, which helped keep me safe. I hung around with my friends from church and did lots of woodworking in school, which got me the award for the best project! I also got a part-time job at "Kelly's Corner" as the head cashier, which I kept for 3 years.

I got drafted in the summer of 1966, which in itself was no big deal, but no way did I want to go to Vietnam. So I went to Puerto Rico, but the government started looking for me. My father responded to their letter and then there I was in the service. I was sent to Fort Jackson and then Fort Gordon for my advanced training. They told me I was going to be a medic, which I convinced them that I couldn't do because of the blood. They accepted that and I was assigned to the Signal Corps.

I first landed in Vietnam in September of 1967. I was so nervous and it was so hot, sticky, and smelly that I threw-up for the first 2 weeks, but finally I settled-down and all I wanted was to do my time and get home. That somehow never really happened completely. I still have my original hard hat, and whenever I hear helicopters or things that sound like them, it all comes back to me. It is like I am back in the Tet Offensive, which had broken-out like all hell, so much so that when I got back to my base camp from Saigon, it was all gone!

When I finally got discharged, which meant turning down a steak dinner and a $1,000 bonus to re-up, I went to PR where my family had returned to. I surprised them, but in 2 weeks, went back to Philly, where I was lucky to get married and have 3 great kids. I was also blessed to get hired by PECO, where I worked in a great job for 28 years.

I guess most folks know of my cousin, John, who they called "The Candyman." He pitched 18 years in the big leagues, including for both the Yankees and the Mets. He could throw in the high 90s and some said he was among the best pitchers ever, having pitched a no-hitter and won a World Series. But when I look back on my life, I think I was pretty much a winner too.

THE WATCH

We lived in North Philly in a close-knit neighborhood at 2212 Jefferson, 235 W. Oxford, and 550 N. 28th Street. These were two-story row homes.

I attended Reynolds Elementary School at 23rd and Jefferson which was close by. My best friend was Isaac Johnson, who we called, "Ike."

For junior high, I went to Vaux Jr. High which was a 5-block walk. I was still friends with Ike.

I went to Edison High school by bus, Route 57, or my dad took me. Mr. Weinberg taught social studies and was my favorite.

My dad was an auto mechanic. He was strict. When we lived on Jefferson Street, and I was 15, and I had just started Edison, he died. To help out, my two uncles moved in briefly.

I graduated and worked at Kline's Coat, Towel & Apron Service for one year. Then I got a letter that I was about to get drafted, so I figured I would enlist.

I told my mom, and she said, "Are you sure that's what you want to do?"

I went to Broad and Cherry where they didn't have to talk me into anything. I picked the Marines because they were elite. Two weeks later, I was getting on a train to Paris Island for boot camp. I was with eight guys that I knew including Nelson Andrews and Ray Douglas.

Basic training was scary, exciting, and made you proud all at once. It was a totally new environment and everybody was afraid of the unknown. After, I went to Camp Geyer, North Carolina for four weeks where I got up close and personal with my M14. If you didn't qualify with your weapon, you got sent to the kitchen to learn to cook.

I made "PFC" right out of boot camp. There must have been something significant that I did, but I don't know what. I'm a little foggy about it.

Then on May 15, 1968, at Kam Lo, I was wounded trying to take a hill when a grenade hit my helmet and sliced my ear. I went to the hospital, then back to my unit and was awarded two Purple Hearts.

In June '68 I was in the 2nd Squad, 3rd Platoon, 3rd Battalion, 4th Marines. Then, I was in the hospital in NY after the recovery from service-related injuries to my arm and ear. I was in a hospital ship for a week, then Guam for a month.

After being in-country from December 16, 1967, to June 15, 1968, going home snuck up on me. I went to Alaska, Japan, and then St. Alban's Naval Hospital, to wean me off pain medication. I also had a second surgery skin graft from my hip and they put a rod in to relieve nerve pain, and I had an operation to fix bones that fused together. My hand felt like it was on fire.

In addition to my injuries, I had some odd situations. Mom and Dad had daughters from previous marriages. One daughter had a son who was a captain, and he got hepatitis and was in the same hospital in St. Albans, New York and they called me up to his floor. He was 30 and had a birthday.

The other weird thing was about this watch I had. I liked different watches. Grey face, orange numbers, and hands. I had lost it on patrol. I got out of the column to tie my shoe, and I see a guy walk by me with my watch on. I had to get the platoon sergeant to get my watch back, but I did get it.

I was discharged on January 31, 1969, after two months in the VA hospital. Then I worked for NE Dodge as a new car detail man. Then I became a Commonwealth of PA Veteran's Employment Representative for 33 years. I was still in touch with my friends Jenkins, Andrews, and Nelson.

I would help vets get jobs and explain how the process works. I started at the Job Center. The Unemployment Center was in the same place. Some of the guys who were collecting unemployment compensation came to see me and got a job. It's called an "OE" "Obtained Employment" by giving info, taking them through the services and referring them to a job. A lot of guys we referred, got employment. I guess I helped thousands of vets.

I met Darlene, my wife of 31 years, at work. Our daughter, Latoya, is 35 and my son, Marcus, is 25, and I learned to play the vibraphone, doing such tunes as "My Favorite Things" and "Contemplation."

Were it not for my family, my job and my music, the post-traumatic stress would have gotten me for sure instead of things turning out okay like with my watch.

Chapter Six

Lost but not Forgotten—
The Edison 64

Almost a half-century has passed since the sixty-four fine young men gave their lives for their Country and Edison High School became known as the school that lost the most to the War. Despite the continued efforts of Dr. Darryrl Johnson, I could locate only a few relatives of those fallen heroes. You will find, therefore, in addition to their interviews, the Official Silver Star Citation of medical corpsman Stephen Paul Blanchett and a narrative of Lural Lee Blevins, with due credit to Chuck Newal, author of *Fearful Odds*.

Following is that material and the photographs of each of the Edison 64. Credit for these is attributed to the Vietnam Veterans Memorial Fund. Photos that required clarity have been retouched on an as needed and best efforts basis.

JOHN EDWARD ADDISON
Date of Birth: 11-3-1948
Date of death: 12-27-1967

JAMES J. ALLEN
Date of Birth: 11-3-1949
Date of Death: 6-5-1968

CHARLES J. ANTONELLY
Date of Birth: 5-31-1945
Date of Death: 11-6-1965

WILLIAM B. BLACKMON, JR.
Date of Birth: 8-26-1950
Date of Death: 1-17-1971

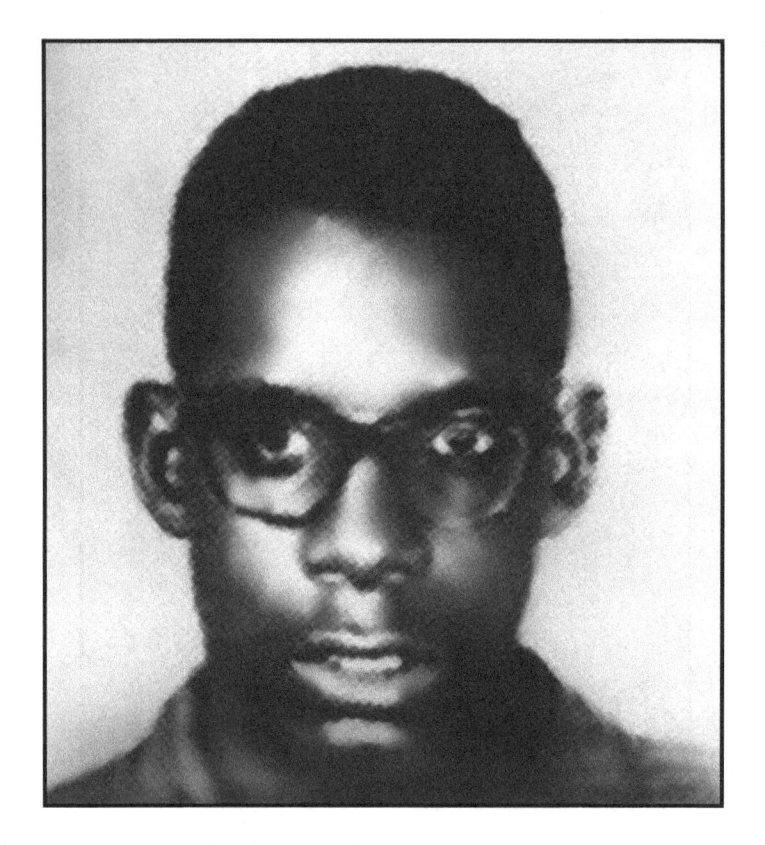

STEPHEN P. BLANCHETT
Date of Birth: 10-20-1947
Date of Death: 3-7-1967

Lural L. Blevins, III
Date of Birth: 11-25-1945
Date of Death: 8-16-1968

Zackrie Brookins, Jr.
Date of Birth: 3-11-1944
Date of Death: 12-31-1966

HECTOR W. BRYAN
Date of Birth: 12-16-1945
Date of Death: 4-1-1966

SAMUEL N. BURTON
Date of Birth: 9-5-1950
Date of Death: 2-12-1970

Robert J. Campbell
Date of Birth: 8-7-1941
Date of Death: 12-21-1965

GLENN CARTER
Date of Birth: 6-10-1949
Date of Death: 9-10-1968

Richard A. Carter
Date of Birth: 2-13-1944
Date of Death: 6-30-1967

WILLIAM CHAPMAN, JR.
Date of Birth: 12-4-1942
Date of Death: 5-15-1968

Milton G. Clayborne
Date of Birth: 12-7-1948
Date of Death: 5-16-1968

Louis A. Cobarrubio
Date of Birth: 6-1-1948
Date of Death: 8-17-1967

DEIGHTON A. DANIELLES
Date of Birth: 5-29-1947
Date of Death: 9-10-1967

Wayne Dillman
Date of Birth: 5-28-1947
Date of Death: 2-8-1968

Lost but not Forgotten—The Edison 64

HAROLD A. DOMAN
Date of Birth: 4-18-1947
Date of Death: 11-26-1967

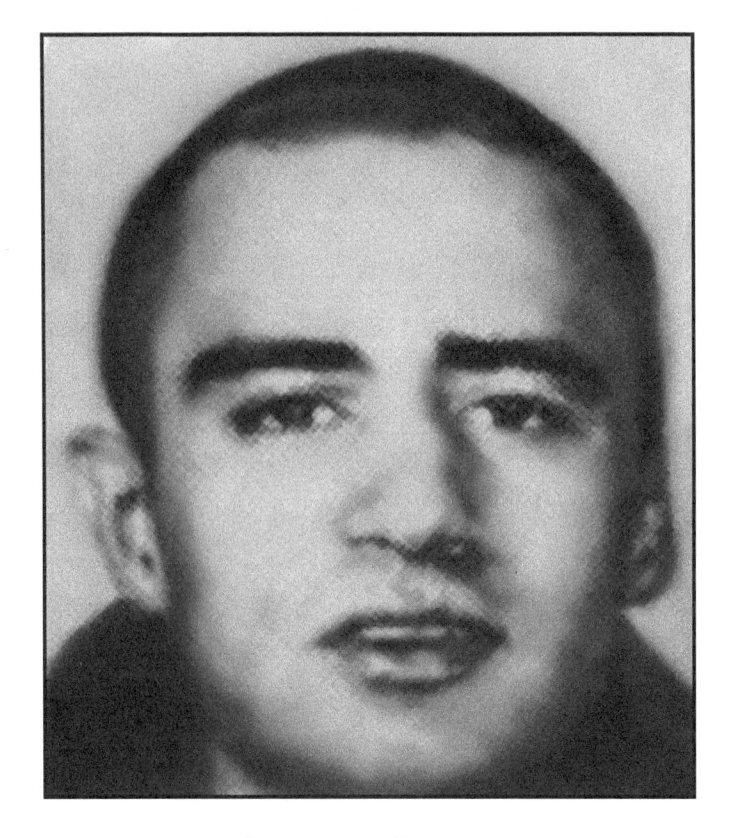

Antonio Garcia
Date of Birth: 3-22-1948
Date of Death: 3-5-1969

CHARLES J. GLENN, III
Date of Birth: 6-25-1947
Date of Death: 7-7-1967

Roscoe Glover, Jr.
Date of Birth: 11-28-1948
Date of Death: 9-22-1968

Lost but not Forgotten—The Edison 64 131

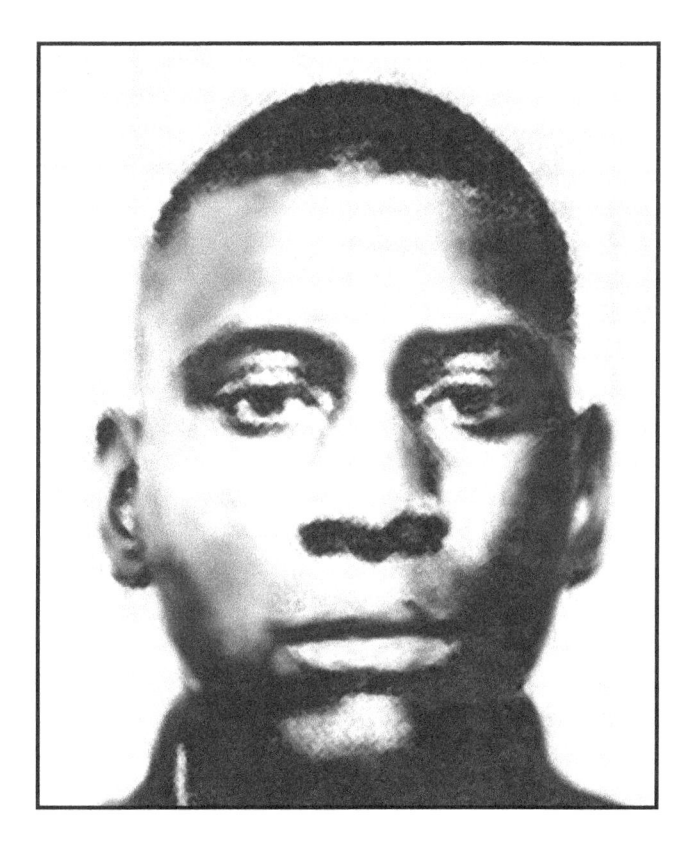

IRVIN J. HOPKINS
Date of Birth: 8-5-1941
Date of Death: 9-30-1966

Rocco R. Isaac
Date of Birth: 4-6-1949
Date of Death: 7-26-1968

RANDOLPH T. JEFFERSON
Date of Birth: 4-17-1950
Date of Death: 7-17-1968

JOSEPH JOHNSON, JR.
Date of Birth: 2-7-1947
Date of Death: 12-22-1968

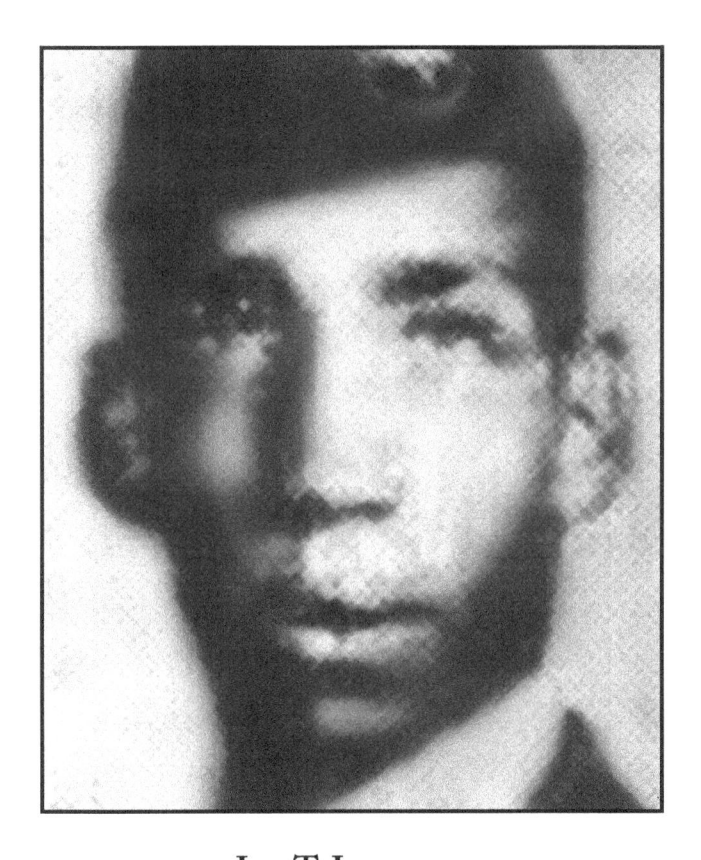

JOE T. JOHNSON
Date of Birth: 12-7-1947
Date of Death: 9-22-1966

JOHN W. JOLLEY, JR.
Date of Birth: 3-3-1947
Date of Death: 9-21-1966

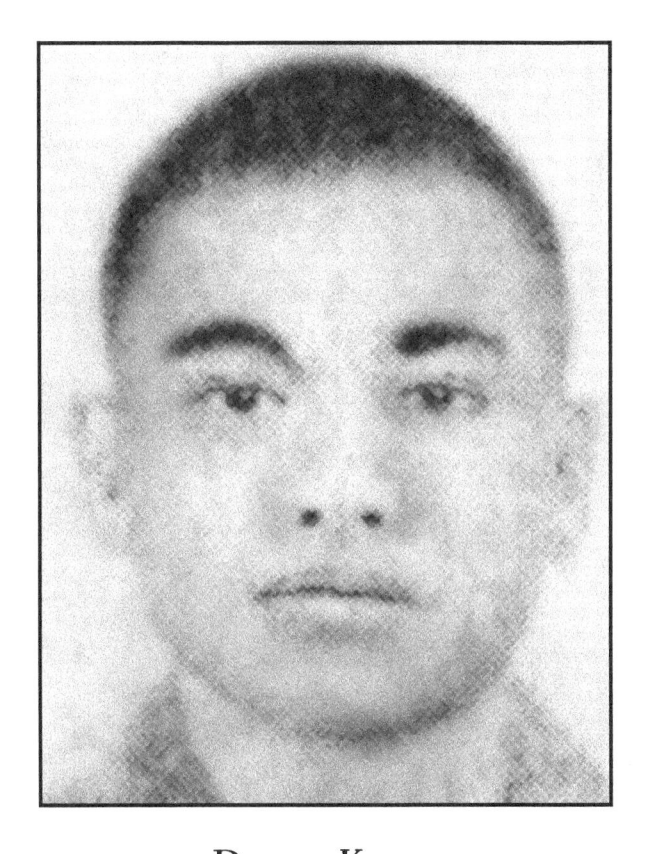

Dennis Kuzer
Date of Birth: 5-11-1947
Date of Death: 7-30-1967

KENNY E. LASSITER
Date of Birth: 7-27-1950
Date of Death: 8-12-1969

Joseph F. Lodise, Jr.
Date of Birth: 9-14-1947
Date of Death: 5-1-1968

GERALD J. MAGUIRE
Date of Birth: 11-24-1946
Date of Death: 1-30-1967

George R. Martin
Date of Birth: 9-11-1949
Date of Death: 3-24-1968

Adolfo Martinez
Date of Birth: 11-6-1948
Date of Death: 2-27-1969

RICHARD F. MCNICHOLS
Date of Birth: 7-6-1944
Date of Death: 7-21-1966

Joseph Mieczkowski
Date of Birth: 9-20-1947
Date of Death: 4-30-1967

Harry James Miller
Date of Birth: 9-25-1927
Date of Death: 1-21-

WILLIAM J. MOORE
Date of Birth: 12-22-1947
Date of Death: 2-22-1967

JOHN G. ORSINO
Date of Birth: 6-28-1949
Date of Death: 10-26-1967

Leroy W. Peagler
Date of Birth: 11-14-1941
Date of Death: 1-27-1967

Lost but not Forgotten—The Edison 64 149

Kenneth Pettus
Date of Birth: 8-15-1948
Date of Death: 3-30-1967

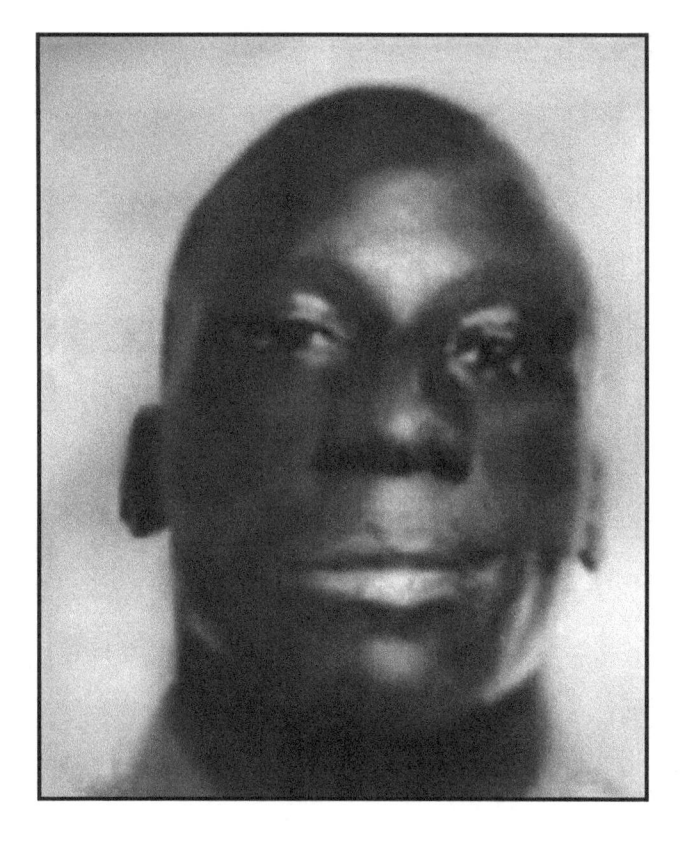

ALFRED A. PURVIS
Date of Birth: 6-6-1950
Date of Death: 2-22-1969

Lawrence J. Reichert
Date of Birth: 9-25-1946
Date of Death: 4-15-1967

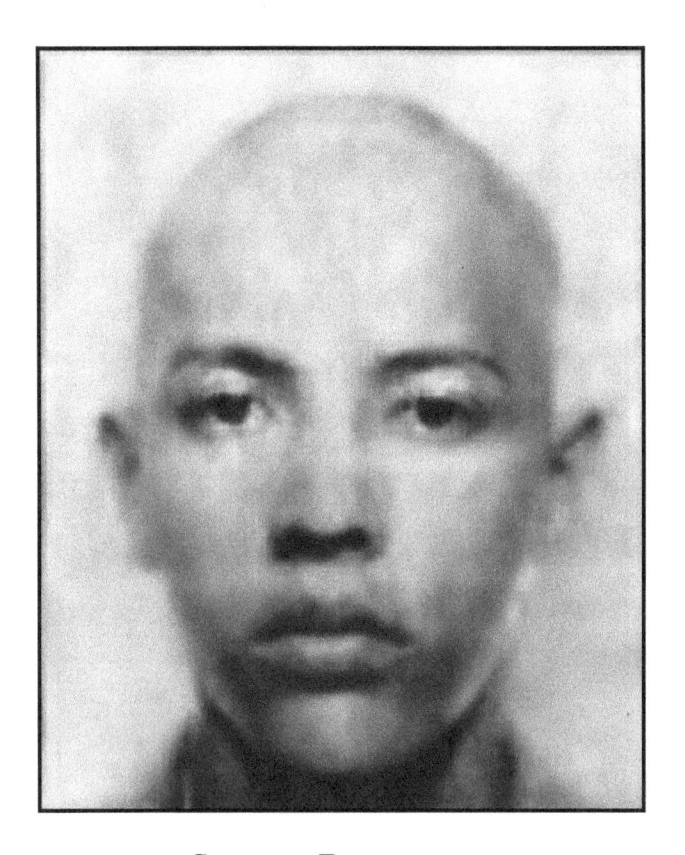

Samuel Rodriquez
Date of Birth: 5-18-1949
Date of Death: 1-29-1969

Lost but not Forgotten—The Edison 64 153

Angelo C. Santiago
Date of Birth: 10-14-1945
Date of Death: 6-6-1968

HARRY B. SEEDES III
Date of Birth: 11-5-1948
Date of Death: 3-3-1969

Darnay Shubert
Date of Birth: 2-22-1949
Date of Death: 12-27-1967

NEELY J. SINGLETARY
Date of Birth: 1-17-1948
Date of Death: 5-11-1967

Lost but not Forgotten—The Edison 64 157

MARK SMITH, JR.
Date of Birth: 1-21-1945
Date of Death: 5-18-1967

JAMES T. SWIFT, JR.
Date of Birth: 8-27-1948
Date of Death: 4-27-1970

HENRY B. THOMAS
Date of Birth: 6-26-1950
Date of Death: 8-31-1970

Aaron L. Thomas
Date of Birth: 12-1-1947
Date of Death: 11-4-1966

Lost but not Forgotten—The Edison 64 161

John J. Thomas
Date of Birth: 9-8-1946
Date of Death: 5-5-1967

Robert Torres
Date of Birth: 3-14-1947
Date of Death: 2-5-1968

Gerald J. Wahlen
Date of Birth: 12-13-1944
Date of Death: 3-28-1967

SAMUEL F. WALKER, JR.
Date of Birth: 7-10-1942
Date of Death: 12-13-1968

Samuel Walker is Missing In Action, or "MIA", which means that he was killed, but neither his remains nor grave have been identified.

Lost but not Forgotten—The Edison 64 165

Nathaniel Washington
Date of Birth: 7-9-1947
Date of Death: 12-13-1965

Joseph A. Weber
Date of Birth: 4-23-1950
Date of Death: 2-24-1969

Lewis N. Welsh
Date of Birth: 7-3-1944
Date of Death: 5-17-1966

GENERAL WHITE
Date of Birth: 8-11-1946
Date of Death: 3-24-1966

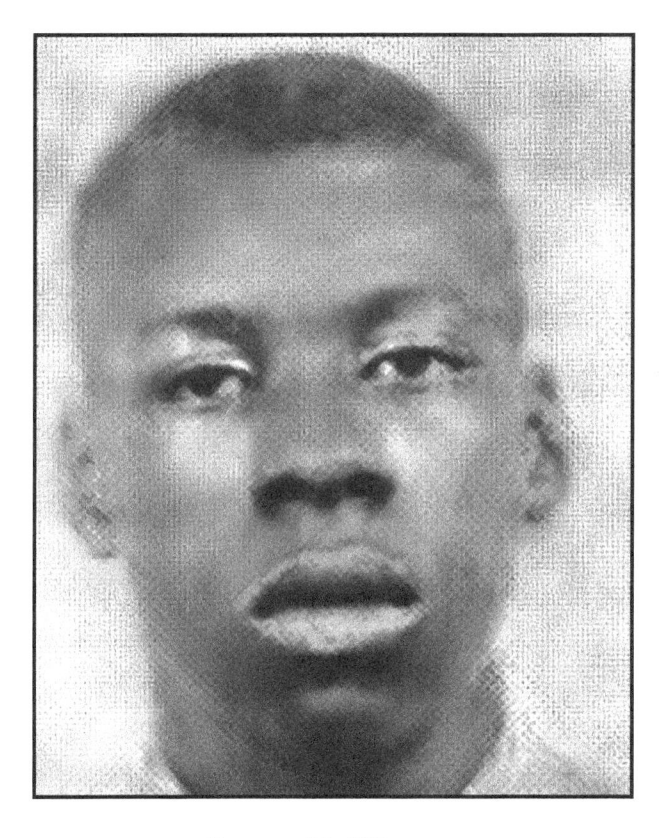

Lost but not Forgotten—The Edison 64 169

JAMES B. WHITE
Date of Birth: 3-20-1942
Date of Death: 2-2-1969

Michael M. White
Date of Birth: 3-1-1948
Date of Death: 6-12-1968

Duane Gregory Williams
Date of Birth: 1-14-1951
Date of Death: 1-1-1970

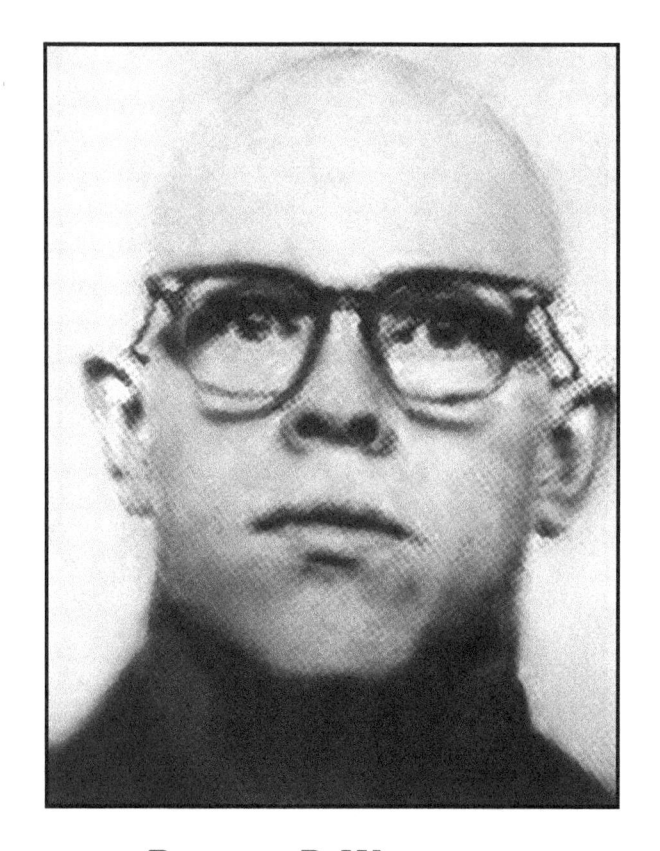

BERNARD R. WOEHLCKE
Date of Birth: 9-7-1948
Date of Death: 12-7-1968

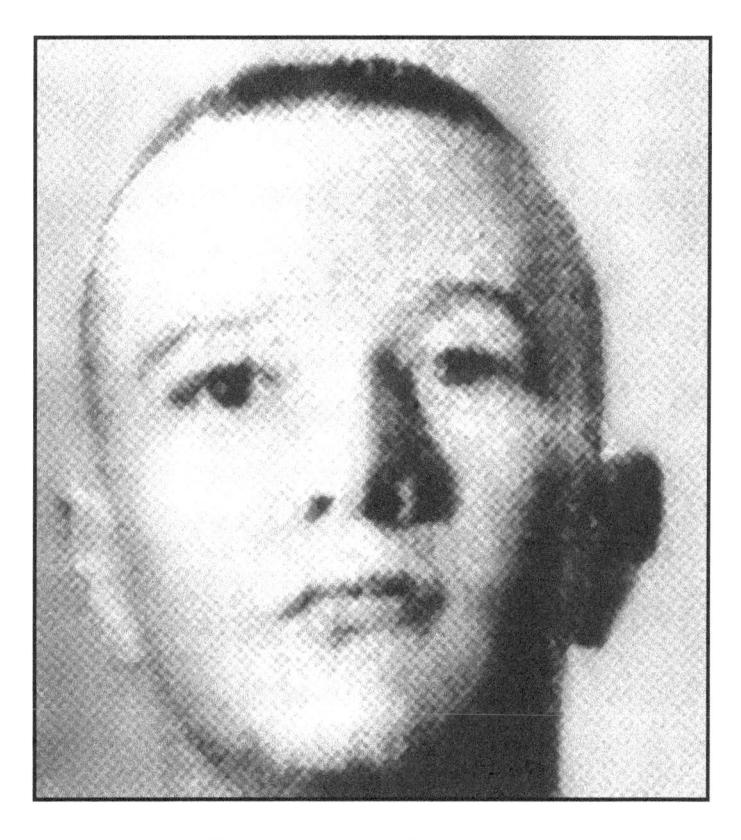

Francis A. Zerggen
Date of Birth: 9-25-1951
Date of Death: 11-20-1970

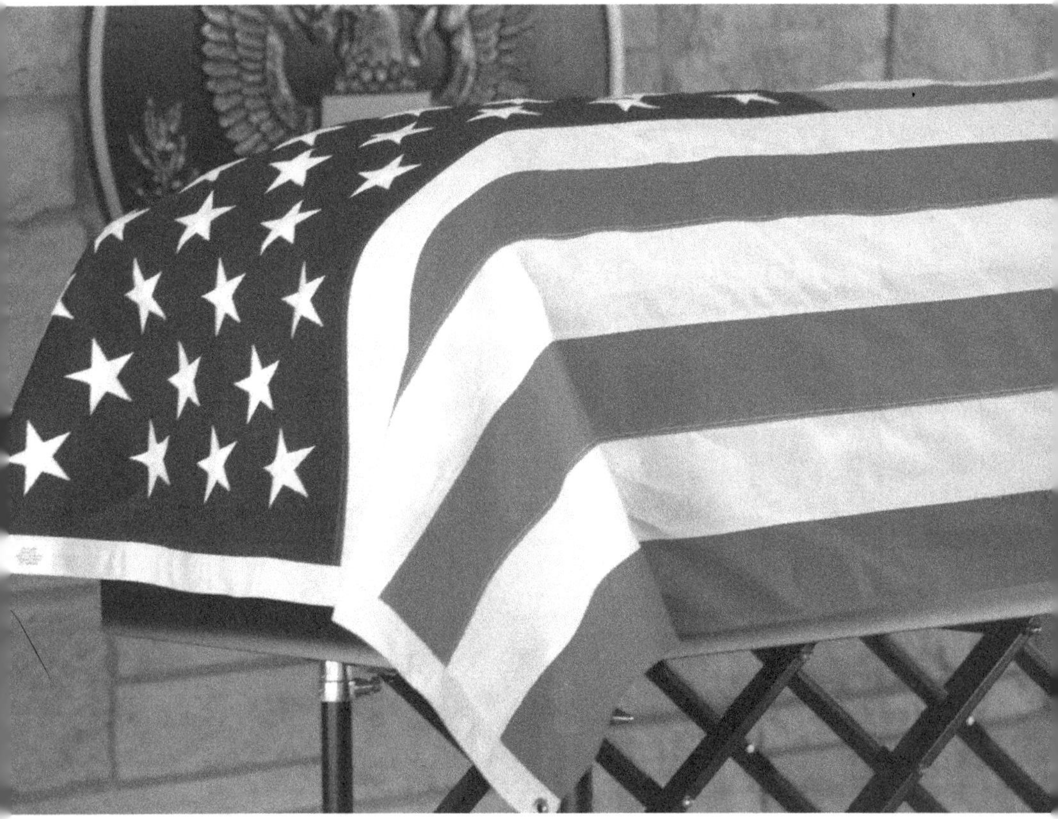

Chapter Seven

Remembrances of Those who Gave their Lives

THE GENTLE GIANT

Based upon interviews with his surviving sister,
Donna Swift Plummer

It wasn't Corporal James Swift, Jr. who was killed in action of August 27, 1970. It wasn't E-4 James Theabert Swift of the 4th Infantry Division of the United States Army who lost his life in Binh Dinh, South Vietnam. It was my big brother.

My family called him, Jake. He was my "gentle giant," so even-tempered and such a good brother. He was older than me, and so big, 6'5", I would say. I grew up with my dad, James Swift, Sr., my mon, Francis, my big brother, James, whom we called Jake, my next brother, Jonto, called Butch, and our little brother, Teddy, whose full name was Julian Theodore. He was only two years old when Jake went off to war.

We lived at 2536 N. Sartain Street right in the middle of the block. Our row house was two stories, and we had a basement, which was good. Our home was built in 1920 and had six rooms altogether, including three bedrooms. It was between 11th and 12th Street and you could walk to the train station.

Where we lived was called North Philadelphia, but we called it "North Philly" and it really was what "The City of Brotherly Love" was and mostly still is, except for what they now call 'gentrification.' What I mean is, it is neighborhoods of families living in row houses, surrounded by other families doing the same. There was the neighborhood store where you could buy milk, bread, and lunch meat and run a tab if you were "short," which we never were because my father worked so hard. And we knew everybody nearby, and when a stranger came along, somebody would ask him what he was doing there.

There wasn't any supermarket or shopping center anywhere nearby, but a few blocks away, there also was a drug store where you called the pharmacist, "Doc," and he could tell you what to do if you asked him. The gangs were still at it, so you had to be careful, but for some reason, we never got bothered, which was just as much luck as anything else.

I don't think it was an exaggeration to say that my brother, Jake, was the best of all of us. Edison High School was all boys like Ben Franklin and Central. Even so, my big brother was able to do so many things well. He earned varsity letters in three sports: football, track, and fencing. I didn't really understand fencing, never having seen it before, but Jake, he told me, it was more planning and thinking than pirates were in the movies or like Zorro was.

He was in the Civil Air Patrol too, he told me, where they taught you about leadership and following orders, and also about flying and space. As much as anything, my "gentle giant" loved music. He played the piano and saxophone like he was born to do it, whether it was jazz or rhythm and blues, or sometimes music he just made up. But what he really did best, better than anything else, was being my big brother.

The story about my first pair of "big girl" shoes is an example of that, although he did lots of other things, like help me with my school work and make sure nobody in the neighborhood or anywhere else, gave me any trouble.

The thing about the shoes was that the ones I was wearing were black and white, like "saddle shoes," but they were flats, without any heels at all. I wanted to wear shoes with heels, even low ones, so I wouldn't feel so much like a kid. My father said it was up to my mother, and my mother said the ones I was wearing were "just fine."

My big brother saw how unhappy I was, and I know he must have talked to Mom because there was no way he would do anything behind her back. Anyway, one day he said to me that tomorrow he's "taking me up to the Avenue," which I could guess meant Germantown Avenue, which was where all the stores were, including the shoe store!

I was so excited about the thought of those shoes with the "kitten heels," which is what they called the ones I asked for. But I was worried too, which I'm pretty sure now was about growing up. I worried about where the money was going to come from and getting in trouble with my parents.

So, after dinner when Jake and Butch were playing stickball in the street, I got my big brother's attention. I'm not really sure how but I did.

"Time!" he said as he brought the game to a halt and came over to the stoop where I was sitting. One of the other kids had something to say, but Jake turned around and gave him a look which made him not say another word.

"Dana, you okay?" my gentle giant said.

I just shook my head. "Yes," I answered, but he knew I wasn't.

"Everything is good, little sister. Now you just stay right here," he told me. "And if you need me, just say so. Meanwhile, I'm going to end this game with the longest home run you ever saw, and then we can talk all you want." He started back to the other kids and then turned around. "I'm going to make Willie Mays jealous," which I figured was a good thing.

The pitcher, who lived across the street, pitched the ball, which was a "pimple ball" we called it because it had little bumps on it and you played with it cut in half. Jake hit it almost into the next block, and I started to cry for some reason. Then after all the kids left, we went for a walk. I really wanted him to hold my hand, but I knew that was too much.

"What's wrong, little sister?" he said.

I shook my head, but when he started to ask me again, I asked him if we were really going tomorrow.

"We are, Dana, we are. Ten o'clock when I'm back from delivering my papers, we're going up to the Avenue. Mom said it's okay since the money's coming from my paper route, which is what a big brother's for."

And the next day we did. The shoes were just what I wanted, and I felt so happy having them and Jake. I have never forgotten that time. It was like magic.

Jake did good in high school, too, even with all his activities and his paper route, and he was popular with the boys and girls, what with how big and nice he was, but it was hard for him to get a job for after graduation. He tried SKF where Daddy worked. They made ball bearings, but there were a lot of people ahead of him. Then TastyKake on Hunting Park Avenue and The Budd Company, which made cars and trains, and even subway cars for the El, but there was nothing there either.

Then he tried a bunch of other places like the department stores which were Lits, Gimbels and Snellenbergs, and a lumber yard and even the grocery store in the neighborhood and on the Avenue and Broad Street, but there was nothing for him. Jake knew he had to do something, so he went into the Army. "The service," my father called it.

Soon, the whole family made the short trip to N. Broad Street where James Swift, Jr., my big brother, joined the Army. After he was inducted, I learned it was called, he was sent to Fort Lewis near Tacoma, Washington. I looked it up later and learned that it had been built almost fifty years before when it was called "Camp Lewis," and now it was where Army soldiers came and went from.

Soon, my big brother, who played the saxophone and the piano and did fencing and football and track and bought me my first big girl shoes, was on his way to the other side of the world.

Butch told me Jake was in the 4th Infantry Division's 704th Maintenance Battalion and was going to Pleiku. His Battalion's motto was "Skilled and Steadfast," but none of that meant anything to me, except that he was so far away.

Everything went okay, because Jake wrote us letters, and we knew he'd be coming home when he got "leave" they called it. We were all so happy to see him, and he told us some about his battalion which he said went all the way back to 1943, which was in World War II, which I didn't know anything about. He also told us that they provided "direct support" for the rolling stock and equipment, but I didn't understand that, either.

What I did get was when Jake was home "on leave" that he was wearing an earring and when I saw that, I just started crying for some reason, even more than before, although I really don't know why I went on so much. He finally took it out and promised not to wear it again.

Jake and Butch spent a lot of time together, and they decided that when he got out of the Army, "discharged" it was called, they would move down South to where the family originally was from. It was beautiful down there, and maybe they could both find work or start a business of some kind. And it wasn't going to be so long from now because he only had a few months left and pretty soon he would be "short," which meant he would have hardly no time at all. I must say I found that kind of funny, his being my "gentle giant," but we were all so happy he'd be home to all of us soon.

That's not what happened. After Jake went back to the Army, we got a letter from somebody high up, saying that Jake was hurt, but that he was recovering from his injuries that we later heard were when the truck he was in drove over a mine. We were all upset waiting for him to get better, hoping and praying, but that's not what happened, either.

One day, my mother looked out the window and there were two soldiers, one black and one white. She knew the horrible, horrible thing right away and started yelling, "You killed my baby! You killed my baby!"

The two soldiers came in and told my mom that Jake was dead. Butch and I tried to do something, but it was too awful. Butch called my father at work, and he had to come all the way from SKF on public transportation knowing that his son was dead.

It took two weeks for my big brother's body to get home. My Uncle Sylvester, who was a captain, accompanied it. Mom couldn't bring herself to go identify the body, which was just as well because we learned later that Jake had lost an arm and leg and part of his head.

When Uncle Sylvester got here, he told us that Jake was probably dead when they sent us the first letter which didn't much matter to me. The funeral at Nimmons over near Broad and Lehigh was so sad and then there was the burial at Arlington Cemetery. There were lots of flags and a ceremony, which I guess was to make you proud, but it only made me so sad that my big brother was in the ground in Virginia with all those graves around instead of home in our living room.

Nobody could say much. We were hurt so bad. My dad, who was a very strong man, was upstairs a couple of weeks after, and he just started wailing. I had never heard a sound like that before or even my father crying at all. But it was him who said it best when he was able to, years later. What mattered to us was not the medals or the ceremonies or my gentle brother's name on the wall, but what my father said: "The War. It took him from us." And as I think about my big brother, Jake, that fine young man, the pride of all of us, the joy of our family, so it did.

BOBBY TORRES

As told by his brother, Raul

My family originally came from Puerto Rico. When I was young, seven or so, we lived in Hoboken, New Jersey and then in New York City on 172nd Street. My dad was the "super" of four buildings, and I remember playing stickball with a "halfie" which was a ball cut in half.

Then we moved to Philadelphia and lived at 610 W. Diamond Street. There were my parents, me, my brothers, Wilfred and Roberto, who was later called "Bobby," and my little sister, Marie. My father worked in a factory four blocks away and sometimes drove a truck. Mom took care of the house. We were involved in the Methodist Church, and I made some friends there.

I went to Edison High School for a year and a half, which I enjoyed because my English was good. Then there was this wonderful principal, Dr. Robert Clarke. He was strict, but he cared about the students and always said, "I love you, boys."

Not that there weren't challenges because the school was black, white, and Latino and the kids formed cliques. The white kids were from Kensington were the ones who had money, which you could tell because they wore shoes to school, and I had these cheap, black sneakers.

I did well in school because I worked hard at it and because I had two languages now. I thought I might become an interpreter for the government. Then it turned out that I was selected as Valedictorian of my class, which was a great honor.

My class guidance counselor suggested I become a teacher, and I was awarded a partial scholarship to Temple University. I paid for the rest of my expenses by working at the Acme supermarket.

I enrolled in the College of Education, hoping to become a language or math teacher. But when I graduated four years later, jobs were hard to come by because guys were using teaching to get deferments from the Vietnam War.

After some waiting, even though I was first on the list, I was offered a job at George Washington High School, which I accepted even though I had no idea where "The Northeast" was. Well, it was two buses and the El away!

The school housed grades 7–12 because they were building a middle school whose students I taught until the building was finished. I taught language for a long time and also pursued my advanced studies at night, earning my M.Ed. in 1969 and then my principal's certificate.

In 1981, I was a department head and then assistant principal at Overbrook and Stetson. Then I applied to be an assistant to the District 5 Superintendent whom I served for a number of years until I got hired as a principal at Edison.

My family life was progressing also. I was blessed to meet my beloved wife, Ruth, in church, and we were married. Then we were fortunate enough to have a son we named Robert.

At the same time, I was falling in love with Ruth, my younger brother was at Community College. Bobby was also working at a pharmacy at Norris and Germantown Avenue. He wanted to be a pharmacist and had a mentor, Sidney Adelman, who was later murdered in a robbery.

However, Bobby's draft lottery number was getting closer and closer, so in March 1966, the same year I got married, he enlisted in the Army. My mom was very upset, but at least he was sent to Germany. Family was the most important thing to her. On Sunday, we would go to church and then have the family dinner that she prepared. Soup, chicken (that I had gotten from the live poultry store) and rice, fresh vegetables. And there was always some extra if we had a visitor.

There were lots of things I remember about our family life. Bobby loved to spend time with Marie, and from the front of our house, you could smell the doughnuts from the Dawn Drive-in. And when the Good n' Plenty factory was operating, you could smell the licorice. Those were the best times.

It was also so nice when Ruth and I were living on Frontenac Street. I was in education and she was working at INA. It's funny now, but I remember thinking if we had a combined income of ten thousand dollars, we would "have it made." Meanwhile, my little brother had been promoted to sergeant and was safe in Germany, and he wrote that he's also coming home for Christmas.

Then, before we know it, my kind and gentle brother, Bobby is in Vietnam in January. He was a team leader with Company C of the 5th Battalion of the 9th Infantry Division. He was killed on February 5, 1968, during the Tet offensive at a place called Long An. I read somewhere that "small arms fire" took his life, but we were told that he had stepped on a mine and then bled to death.

I went with my father to the funeral home, and then we had the service at the 7th Street Methodist Church. Bobby went back home and was buried in the Bayamon National Cemetery in Puerto Rico.

We were all devastated of course, but my mother particularly. She completely withdrew into herself and wouldn't even watch TV. My mother wouldn't get counseling or anything like that, so my parents tried moving back to Puerto Rico to be there near their son, I guess.

That didn't work either and my mom fell into a long period of deep depression. Eventually, my father and mother divorced. My father worked in the resort hotels on the island and sometime during this horrible part of our lives, my brother Wilfred was murdered by his wife.

Somehow, I was able to push on despite my terrible guilt that it wasn't I who went to Vietnam. But I became principal of the school that I attended and dedicated myself to give back as had been given to me.

That part of my life worked out pretty well. We had lots of activities like sports and theater, and the students were getting into college.

After more than 30 years of service, I took an early-out package. I had spent 16 years in the classroom and 16 years in administration. We sold our house in Castor Gardens, and I took a job at Whole Foods where I became an assistant manager.

We moved to New Jersey, and my son and daughter live in Maryland. I survived aortic aneurysm surgery and am back working. But my guilt and sadness will always be with me.

STEPHEN PAUL BLANCHETT

Stephen came from a large family, which included six siblings. He entered the Army in November of 1964 and was engaged to be married at the time. In addition to attending Edison, he was active in his church.

He was awarded the Silver Star as described officially below. It was given posthumously:

The President of the United States, authorized by Act of Congress July 9, 1918, (amended by an act of July 25, 1963) takes pride in presenting the Silver Star (Posthumously) to Private First Class Stephen Paul Blanchett (ASN 12728274), United States Army, for gallantry in action while engaged in military conflict against an armed hostile force in the Republic of Vietnam while serving with Headquarters and Headquarters Company 3rd Battalion, 60th Infantry Regiment, 9th Infantry Division, Private First Class Blanchett distinguished himself by exceptional valor while service as Medical Specialist for his unit when it came under heavy small arms fire in rice paddies, northwest of Dong Tam, Vietnam on 7 March 1967. As the unit was maneuvering slowly through several rice paddies, they came under enemy sniper file. Immediately, one of the unit's leaders was hit and severely wounded. Private Blanchett, 350 meters to the rear, was notified and began racing through the paddies in order to reach the wounded man. When he had come to within 50 meters of the casualty, fellow comrades urged him to go no further, due to the increasing amount of hostile fire. He courageously disregarded the warning and with fire all about him, ran to the side of the wounded man. He then pulled the wounded man behind the safety of a dike separating two paddies and administered vitally needed first aid. This courageous act was one of many times he unhesitatingly risked his life in behalf of his fellow soldiers.

Private First-Class Blanchett's extraordinary heroism in close combat against a numerically superior Viet Cong force was in keeping with the highest traditions of military service and reflects great credit upon himself, the 9th Infantry Division and the United States Army."

My Brother, Gerry Maguire

As told by his sister, Denise Maguire Gubicza

Our dad was in World War II, like his brother, Adam. It was real rough on him and us kids, Joe, Gerry and my younger sister, Maria. Lots of times Dad would be screaming about the Germans and sometimes he'd grab me and hold me behind the sofa yelling, "The Nazis are coming! The Nazis are coming." It drove my father to drink and then to be a drunk and not be able to hold a job. Nobody could blame Dad, though, because he landed on that beach on D-Day in World War II.

So, I guess he felt good, or at least as much as he could when the draft board rejected my older brother, Joe, because he had gotten an injury from falling on the ice, and they said that made him unable to serve. Joe got married and had a child, but that "luck" in being rejected turned out to be an awful thing when his younger brother, Gerry, got killed. From that day on, Joe was always saying, "It should have been me. It should have been me."

We lived in Fishtown and then moved to Hancock Street, where my grandfather lived because he needed caring for and that's what families do. We lived in a two-story, three-bedroom house, and Joe and Gerry shared a room like we girls did.

Joe graduated from North Catholic like my husband, Steve, and after graduation worked as a bank teller and then became a Philly cop like Steve did after he served in Vietnam. He was a K-9 cop and loved it and would bring his dog home after we were married.

Since we had moved, my older brother, Gerry, Gerald Joseph, started at Edison High as a teenager. He hated it, but he liked to box and got a reputation as someone who could really handle himself. Not that he was a tough guy or anything.

He was a great big brother and took me to my first baseball game, which was a doubleheader at Connie Mack Stadium. (I thought it would never end.) And when I was ten, to my first movie at a theater near my aunt's house. It was one of those monster movies and when the scary parts came, you could tell by the music, he'd cover up my face, so I wouldn't be scared.

Most of all, he liked basketball, which he played mostly at the Lehigh Avenue Recreation Center or "playground" as we called it. He was very popular and had lots of friends like Joe Higgins and Charlie Townsend. After Edison, he got a job at the Stetson Hat Company where his grandparents worked. Then he was drafted in 1966. My father knew something terrible was going to happen. And on January 30, 1967, it did.

Gerry went into the Army on November 24, 1966, and did his training at Fort Polk, Louisiana. He was a private first-class E-3 in the 8th Calvary of the First Calvary Division. He would write home a lot and say how beautiful "the country" was and ask us to send candy and Kool-Aid for the kids. Gerry was still a very giving person and particularly when it came to kids and animals. He once brought home a kitten, and then a dog and even a parakeet he found in a snowstorm.

On January 30, 1967, when he was twenty and I was sixteen, it all came to an end in a place called Binh Dinh where my brother was shot in the head. Later, a captain came and knocked at our door. My mother screamed, and my father kept saying over and over, "Just tell me he's wounded."

But Gerry was dead. My father drank more and more and got depressed because he thought God took his son because he and his brother had survived World War II. My mother started drinking too, and my brother, Joe, kept saying over and over that it should have been him instead of getting passed-over because of falling on the ice. My younger sister, Maria, who was nine when he died, said she felt cheated that she hadn't gotten to know him more.

I got angrier and angrier and blamed the Army. I was so upset for ten years, I couldn't even say that I had a brother, Gerry, even though he once let me deliver his paper route and who taught me to play ball, my brother, Gerry who would sit with me on the stoop in the hot summer nights, and who I miss every single day, all these years later.

Time does go on. His friends drew up a petition themselves so that the playground was named after Gerry, and it still is. I went on to become a nurse, which I always wanted and best of all, I met and married my husband, Steve, and with God's help, together we got through his Vietnam experiences and the loss of my sweet brother.

SilverHand

As told by Reginald Pollitt

We grew up in the Strawberry Mansion section of Philadelphia, one block from the famous concert venue, "The Dell East." I had 3 brothers, and a sister, Clara. Our dad, who was a veteran of the U.S. Coast Guard, worked at the Liberty Fish Company at the food distribution center and mom worked at the department store, "Sears and Roebuck."

Our family life was a good one in our row house and because there was an alley next to us, there were always neighbors around. My neighbor, Dennis, from back then, is still my friend today. There was always art and music, particularly from "The Dell" and we had an artist paint two big murals in our home.

We went to Walton Elementary School and after we graduated, we followed each other to Fitzsimons Junior High. However, by that time, things were pretty rough because of the gang warring, so a day at school could also mean running into "the 29D's", "Village" or "The Valley," all of which could mean getting hurt or worse.

All of the boys went to Edison and worked with our dad in the fish business whenever they could. My brother, Ronnie, was very good-natured and had a great sense of humor. He was very adventurous and loved anything to do with Indians, including their religion, bow hunting, and Western movies. He was so into Native American culture that he became a great hunter and master bowman himself, and even began referring to himself as "Rondo" or his favorite name, "SilverHand."

So it made sense to us when my big brother gave-up his part-time job at Katz's Luncheonette and enlisted in the Army where he could experience a lot of the same kind of things. This brought him eventually to being stationed at Fort Benning and being a paratrooper in the 101st.

Ronald served in Vietnam for 13 months, but maintained his relationship with the family, writing and sending us pictures. My favorite one was SilverHand in the bush, manning the radio. We had a "Welcome Home, Ronnie" party when he came back, which was something many who served didn't have.

At that time, I was working at Boeing and also going to Temple University and then working at IVB Bank. My big brother though started getting sick from the Agent Orange poisonous defoliant he was exposed to in the War. This developed into squamous cell cancer of his head and neck, for which he treated at Hahnemann University Hospital. Tragically, this disease, which I believe was clearly caused by the Agent Orange, killed my big brother in 2011 when he was 45 years of age and he was buried in North Philadelphia.

While all this was going on, SilverHand and the rest of us thought the Veterans Administration would take care of Ronnie and give him benefits. None of that happened, in spite of many scientific findings linking his type of cancer to Agent Orange. Rather, there was lots of litigation as to causation and entitlement and many like my brother got nothing. To this day, I carry a picture of Ronnie in my wallet and I can't help think about what happened with the American Indians and smallpox.

Products of the Enemy

I grew up around the corner from the older Thomas Edison School and went to junior high at Germantown Avenue and Allegheny. I was a swimmer from 6th grade on and competed in the breaststroke until I graduated Edison in 1968. My favorite subjects were anything that had to do with electricity. My least favorite was anything that had to do with the gangs and their warring, like "11th and Cumberland" and "The Tioga T's."

My family life was marked by my dad being crushed to death in a work accident. However, I was fortunate enough to have his younger brother, "Uncle Henry," being always there for me, like giving me advice, particularly about the importance of education, and coming to the house and taking me to the movies. Also, there was a military tradition in my family, going back to my great, great grandfather who fought in the Civil War. Uncle Henry was in the Vietnam War as was my cousin, Louis Russell Valentine. I had lots of relatives in World War II.

Unfortunately, Uncle Henry, who was a staff sergeant, was killed in action on January 21, 1967 when he was almost forty years old. He was buried in Arlington Cemetery and then brought closer to home to a cemetery in Mount Holly, New Jersey.

My cousin gave his life in Nam in 1969. I am often asked about my feeling about losing my relatives in the war and my close friend, James Swift from Edison. I tell them that soldiers go off to fight, knowing they don't always come back. But, I went in the service in 1968. I wanted to join the Marines to kill the enemy that had killed those close to me.

Fortunately, I took the advice of a family friend and went into the Navy, where I was on the USS Guam, a helicopter landing carrier. More fortunately, I served in the Carribean and not Vietnam.

We had a crew of 2,000 and could carry 4,000 marines. Our sister ship, the Inchon, was stationed on the West Coast.

I had trouble getting a job in Philly when I got home, so I went to New York and took the Civil Service test. This got me the career of working with troubled kids, which I did for 32 years. I was also fortunate to be happily married and my wife and I to be blessed with 5 children, 5 grandchildren, and 3 great-grandchildren.

Still, I still remember how I was washing our windows when I learned about my uncle's death, and I miss those people close to me who died in Vietnam. I also resent how the government handled my GI benefits, and the fact that my Country's going to Vietnam was all about the dollar, from taking over for the French, to doing business with those who used to be our enemies. I had a part-time job in loss prevention after I retired and there they were, boxes of big screen televisions. Stamped on the box was "Product of North Vietnam"!

LURAL LEE BLEVINS III

Lural Lee Blevins, III, or "Earl" as he was known, was from the Frankford part of North Philadelphia and attended Edison High School. He enlisted in the U.S. Army in May of 1966, two months after his marriage to his wife, Brenda.

Literally, days before he was to return to his wife and daughter, Alonda, to pursue a career as a mechanic, Specialist Blevins was killed by a sniper's shot to his head. The tragic event took place four or five kilometers northwest of the village of A Luoi. Contrary to various mottos, his body was left behind.

What we do know of the service and sacrifice is mainly attributable to Charles W. Newhall, III, author of the fine book, *Fearful Odds*. Then Lieutenant Newhall commanded the initial reconnaissance of what is often known as Hamburger Hill in the A-Shau Valley, for which he was awarded the Bronze Star and Silver Star. He went on to earn a degree from the University of Pennsylvania and a Master's from Howard University and then a successful career in business.

Lural Blevins was from Edison High. He was muscular, proud of his heritage, and courageous and skilled at his work as a Spec E-4. Committed to his brother soldiers and Country, he had only two days left in Vietnam but risked and eventually lost his life to those on that hill. This was after saving the lives of his platoon leader and squad leader, pulling them to safety in an attack on a command bunker.

Earl's greatest skill and value was his ability to call in air support with pinpoint accuracy, which made him a great asset. In his last battle, he was calling in the napalm and bombs to save his brothers and replacing the M-60 machine gun by using his M-16.

It was then that he was shot in the forehead by a sniper which killed him instantly. Lural Lee Earl Blevins, III, died for the man on his right and on his left as Newhall tells us at page 82.

To compound the tragedy of the incident, Blevins fell over onto the enemy's side of the hill, and contrary to the commitment to "leave no man behind," his body was not recovered for months, his wife bewailing that not even his wedding ring was brought home.

Moved by the bravery and sacrifice of Blevins, Lt. Newhall submitted his soldier for the Congressional Medal of Honor. These efforts failed, but Newhall was assured that Blevins would be receiving the Distinguished Service Cross for what Lieutenant Ron Christian called his "natural bravery and instinctive disregard of his own safety." This never happened, either. The reason that Blevins was passed over even until this day was that, as a high school student, he had been arrested for stealing a set of hubcaps.

Newhall then reached out to the "Edison 64" who attempted to assist in having a 37-unit building for veterans housing be named for Lural Lee Blevins, III. Despite the dedication and persistence of Edison 64 historian, Dr. Darryrl Johnson, this too failed. Even the efforts of a noted newspaper columnist, Stu Bykofsky, could not initially help this hero who saved the lives of more than 25 of his brothers.

However, on November 10, 2017, a closed school was dedicated in Blevins' name as housing for veterans. Due to the commitment of Congressman Bob Brady, City Councilman Darrell Clarke, Housing Commissioner Kelvin Jeremiah, HELP USA, Philadelphia Veterans Advisory Commission, Chuck Newhall, and Edison Historian Dr. Darryrl Johnson, who made the nomination, the building now stands as a lasting testament to Blevins. And the efforts to have him receive the proper commendations continue.

Chapter Eight

The Deepest Wounds

"There was horror in his dreaming like the terror in his waking. Ashman dreamt that he ran along a long hall with no doors. The hall got narrower and narrower as he ran so that he could not move. The walls and ceilings became each other and pressed down and on him so that he could not breathe. There was no escape.

"New dreams came more awful, more cruel, more cunning. They drenched him with all the terror and horror he had ever known. Bags with severed heads of once good friends, feeding rats, betrayal in the night. Ashman felt himself screaming, but no sound came out."

I have been told that these passages from my novel, *Tunnel Runner*, ring true notwithstanding my being neither a psychiatrist, psychologist nor having served in combat. One must also embrace the relevant and piercing words of Stephen Crane in his classic *Red Badge of Courage*, which was written without the author having ever seen a day of combat. Yet who could not be moved when we hear Henry say, "I can't stand this much longer."

Numerous combat veterans and healthcare professionals have said that the emotions and images in *Tunnel Runner* are appropriate and accurate. On one occasion, for instance, I had to approach the boundaries of rudeness to reject the invitation for lunch from a recently retired CIA operative who could not accept that I had written a book of pure fiction, without my having any experience whatsoever.

You, who are reading this, know that I am speaking the truth if you have war experience. But I do so humbly and not as a participant. I am a vehicle only. My knowledge comes from those who have the experience that comes with facing the deaths of others and of oneself. I am honored to have been entrusted with emotions and secrets and sometimes previously untold stories in my interviews with the Edison veterans. And there are the silent witnesses of our friends and relatives, who have been in "The mud and blood" but never speak about it, which is an undeniable affirmation of the awful memories that their silence hid.

Like many of us, I had my own personal experience witnessing the deeply imbedded self-denial of the lasting post traumatic stress. My father-in-law, "Moe Daley," had dreamt of becoming a veterinarian, but the fact that he was Catholic was an impediment. So, he raised his family, which included six children, by working as a boiler-maker and car salesman. Before that, he served in the United States Navy in the Korean War, of which he had never said a single word at home.

We were all watching football because it was Thanksgiving. We cheered and booed, ate and joked. Then, for the first and only time, he spoke about the war. It was connected to nothing as far as we could tell and just came out, bringing us all to stop our talking and laughing. Somehow, even though Moe Daley was speaking in not more than a quiet tone, we could hear him clearly above the television.

"It was a pitch-black night except for some stars and the lights on our vessel through the water, which was just as black as the sky was. And then the clouds moved from in front of the moon and showed the people in the water and the sharks' fins coming in. And those people were waving their arms around and yelling out, "Help us! Help us!" They called, they screamed. But our CO told us we had to leave them there. Which is what we did."

Then, just as suddenly, my father-in-law was back talking about the football game as if someone else had told that terrible tale. And we were stunned and helpless and could only wonder what it must have felt like for him during that war, and leaving these people to the sharks and what burden and suffering he must have carried for all these years. And he never spoke about the Navy or Korea or anything else like that ever again.

And I know a man whose father did so much killing in World War II that he took to beating his own son, so much that they had run out of hospitals to go to for the kid's "accidents." Another man I knew, a professional man who was well respected, who had spent four years in combat in the South Pacific, once went rushing into the house next door to pummel his next-door neighbor in front of his family. Then there was my friend in high school whose dad would grab his wife and kids and run down to the basement whenever he heard a loud noise

Recognition of the terrible suffering caused by war greatly expanded as a result of Vietnam, and even then, it took a long time, too long. Such as vividly described by Jonathan Shay, MD, Ph.D. Dr. Shay is the psychiatrist for American Combat Veterans with chronic Post Traumatic Stress Disorder. In his *Achilles in Vietnam*, he offers the comments of his patients which I repeat here as a dramatic testament to the reality of PTSD.

"I haven't really slept for twenty years. I lie down, but I don't sleep," says one soldier.

"I've been waiting to die ever since I got back from Vietnam," says a second.

"I'm so envious of all the normal people who can just go to the mall and hold hands with their wife and walk around," another tells us.

"If only I could cry like I did the day he had his face shot off. I haven't cried since then. Never."

Tragically, this kind of suffering went largely ignored after the Vietnam War and did not receive appropriate attention until the 1980s. As far back as the 1700s, it was referred to by Dr. Josef Leopold as "nostalgia" and in the Civil War as "Da Costa's Syndrome." Then came the unscientific terminology "battle fatigue," and in World War II, "shell shock." The term used for the symptoms related to the Korean War was "gross stress reaction."

In all these cases, the conditions were not afforded the appropriate prevention and treatment the symptomatology called for. This understandably resulted in long, even interminable periods of segregation and mind-numbing drugs or the infamous brutality of General Patton, whose science was to slap his "malingerers" during the Sicily campaign. There was no appropriate curative attention until the American Psychiatric Association recognized the condition as Post-Traumatic Stress Disorder (PTSD) in 1980.

The next significant step was the investigation of PTSD in 1983 in response to Congress's mandate, known as "The National Vietnam Veterans Readjustment Study." Those who served during the Southeast Asian Conflict were evaluated as to groups of active duty in the combat zones, elsewhere and non-active personnel. Adjustments were also made as to service duties such as combat, combat support, and service.

The study concluded that over eight hundred thousand service personnel had lifetime Post-Traumatic Stress Disorder, with four-fifths of them suffering recent symptoms. Such symptoms included radical emotional shifts, aggressive acting-out, guilt, helplessness, social avoidance, addictions, anger, relationship deterioration, fear flashbacks, shame, nightmares, hypersensitivity, feelings of betrayal and failure, physical pain, and paranoia.

Subsequent studies are highlighted by The National Vietnam Veterans Longitudinal Study (NVVLS) conducted as a decade's later follow-up. The data collected in 2013–2015 showed that even with adjustments for mortality, 271,000 Vietnam theater veterans still had active Post-Traumatic Stress Disorder, including a significant percentage with major depressive order. The Department of Veterans Affairs adds to this tragic finding by concluding that Vietnam veterans are even now, twice as likely to die earlier than non-combat vets. This includes by disease such as cancer, accidents, suicide, and murder.

The American Journal of Epidemiology explains this, as does researcher Alan Peterson of the Texas Health Science Center, to be a result of the effect of the veteran's post traumatic stress effect on all organs.

The foregoing undeniably leads to the conclusion as set forth in the following: "In War there are no unwounded soldiers," (*Combat Veterans to Careers*) and as stated in the *Journal of Traumatic Stress*, "Combat exposure is the only correlate consistently associated with PTSD."

The direct relationship between War and the decades-lasting suffering of Post-Traumatic Stress Disorder must not be ignored. There are various approaches offered by the Veterans Administration, the armed forces, various non-profits, and a growing number of individual practitioners. While they offer different success rates and it may be said, are all belated, it is of value to examine them for a direction towards success.

Numerous pharmaceuticals are now in use. Included are anti-depressants such as Amitriptyline and Imipramine. Benzodiazepines have some value for PTSD patients with anxiety, irritability, and sleep disturbances. These include Lorazepam, also known as Ativan, and Diazepam, the generic for Valium. Selective Serotonin Uptake Inhibitors such as Lexapro, Prozac, and Zoloft are also prescribed.

While not FDA approved for this specific use, anti-convulsant medication such as Lamictal are often prescribed for patients with post-traumatic impulsivity problems. Alpha-1 Receptor Antagonist drugs are often prescribed for patients to reduce nightmares. These include Prazosin, known as Minipress. It should also be noted that certain drugs known as Alpha-2 adrenergic antagonists, such as Clonidine, have proven to be beneficial in dealing with hyperarousal symptoms of Post-Traumatic Stress Disorder.

An interesting and controversial drug now being used to fight Post-Traumatic Stress is Propranolol, a beta-blocker used primarily to treat high blood pressure, heart problems, and migraines. According to the Journal of Psychiatric Research, it is used to treat PTSD because it blocks the neurotransmitters that enhance memory. It has been used to prevent stage fright. In fact, a 1987 study confirmed that more than one-quarter of those studied admitted using beta blockers to block stage fright. More recently, Harvard psychiatrist, Dr. Roger Pitman, has found that dosing patients with Propranolol before talking about their stress-related events, blocks the re-storage of traumatic incidents. It must be noted that there are ethical and legal questions raised as to pharmaceuticals which alter memory.

The treatment of PTSD now includes an increasing number of non-chemical therapies. These include cognitive and behavioral talking therapy and EMDR, Eye Movement Desensitization and Reprocessing, which is a process using sound or tapping in order to access the traumatic memory network so new emotional and mental associations can be formed. Other non-pharmaceutical approaches include TRE, Trauma Releasing Exercises, meditation, equine assisted treatment, application of Native American rituals and more recently, even the controlled use of marijuana.

Ironically, of the foregoing, the most worthy of note may be the understanding and application of the culture of ancient societies in their treatment of the mental and emotional damage caused by war. Anthropologist Kristofer Plitzkin points to the returning warriors' lack of shame or guilt, which he attributes to the availability of gods and deities available to them.

A like position was proposed by Sebastian Junger, best-selling author of *Tribe-On Homecoming and Belonging*. He writes, "The loss of closeness that comes at the end of deployment may explain the high rates of PTSD suffered by military veterans today."

We should, therefore, take a cultural look at the treatment of soldiers and its effect upon them. In many ancient and less complex societies, the fighters were admitted back to society in stages, which included living outside the city walls. The Greeks offered their soldiers, parades, celebrations, honors, and the comfort of women as antidotes to the horrors of war. The Apaches and Comanches treated their warriors similarly.

This leads us to the present and the work of Dr. Armen Shay. Dr. Shay is a Professor of Psychiatry at the NYU School of Medicine, specializing in the treatment of Post-Traumatic Stress Disorder. He has written in the *Journal of the American Medical Association* that "Chronic PTSD is tenacious and disabling.... Preventing post-traumatic stress disorder is a pressing public need." Similarly, he states in "Psychiatric Clinics of North America," that, "Despite advances in knowledge, PTSD remains prevalent, chronic, disabling and costly."

We must also note his comment in an article written by Sebastian Junger for *Vanity Fair* magazine. Dr. Shay offers his support of the above-referred comment by Junger. In doing so, he offers scientific underpinnings for Junger's position and therefore a key to dealing with the scourge of PTSD.

Shay addressed the remarkably low incidence of Post-Traumatic Stress Disorder among the Israeli Armed Forces or the Israeli Defense Force. He attributes the incidence of approximately 1% to the "shared public meaning of the War." That communal attitude is in stark contrast to the fractured and antagonistic reception that awaited the U.S. combat soldiers when they returned from Vietnam. The choruses of insults still ring loudly, "Baby Killers!"

Our armed forces' approach to combat training exacerbated the effect that the public hatred and insults to our soldiers caused. Although it is not suggested here that the approaches noted before were intentional, there is no doubt that our training methods made fertile ground for PTSD.

This is true in three unique ways. Firstly, as Lt. Col. David Grossman writes in his *The Psychological Cost of Learning to Kill in War and Society*, "The American soldier in Vietnam was first psychologically enabled to kill to a far greater degree than any other soldier in previous history." Next should be noted that the youth of our combat veterans was of an average age less than twenty years. And thirdly, was our armed forces practice of rotating soldiers in and out, which certainly diluted the support of one soldier to another.

So, what are we to do? We must, of course, accept our societal responsibility for the suffering of PTSD caused by the mistreatment of our own soldiers. We must expand our treatment alternatives and regimes, which must be offered quickly and without stigma, and we must undo the lack of pride and appreciation that transmutes itself into a PTSD accelerator.

As I pointed-out in a previous chapter, that as part of my interview process, I asked each veteran if their neighbors knew about

The Deepest Wounds

their sacrifices and accomplishments. Occasionally, one would point out that a neighbor around the block "knew I was in Vietnam."

That is not enough. Neither are the monuments or celebrations on Memorial Day or Veteran's Day. We owe these men, and each day as their suffering eats at them, we owe them even more. Perhaps the annual National Vietnam War Veterans Day, which was signed into law by President Trump to begin on March 29, 2017, after an introduction by Senators Toomey and Donnelly, may affect the psyche of society and then the behaviors towards our Vietnam veterans, including the Edison 64 and their survivors. Perhaps even this book may have some effect. But more must be done.

Chapter Nine

The VA

One of the most common and upsetting things I learned from my interviews of the Vietnam veterans from Edison was the incomprehensible delay in their receipt of the benefits due them. Routinely, I would be told that our servicemen waited decades to receive their due from the United States Department of Veterans Affairs, also known as the Veterans Benefits Administration, the Veterans Administration, or most commonly, "The VA."

Even with the shocking revelations about the numerous scandals at the VA, it is difficult to fathom those who sacrificed and suffered so much would be made to wait so long. Routinely, I would be told by a veteran that he had prostate cancer and diabetes, clearly attributable to his being exposed to our poisonous Agent Orange, who waited more than twenty years for disability benefits. Or they had ischemic heart disease and myeloma from the poisonous defoliant and waited twenty-five years. Or were still suffering from Post-Traumatic Stress Disorder and Parkinson's Disease and were ignored for decades.

How could that be? In some ways, it is so callous and heinous that it doesn't matter what the reasons are. There can be no acceptable excuse or justification, particularly because of our history of care for those who fought to preserve and save our society.

Our heritage of providing for our soldiers even predates the founding of our Country. This tradition goes as far back as the Pequot War of 1636 in which New England colonies joined with the Native American tribes of the Mohicans (or Mohegans) and the Narragansett tribe in defeating the Pequot. Following that conflict, the Pilgrims enacted legislation to support all the disabled soldiers.

This tradition continued with the founding of our country so that those disabled in the Revolutionary War were provided pensions. Then, in 1811, the first veterans care facility was established as the U.S. Naval Asylum in Philadelphia. The federal government expanded its pension system for veterans by the creation of the Bureau of Pensions in 1833.

Then came the General Pension Law to provide benefits for those who were injured in the Civil War. The Civil War also prompted the Soldiers Home, which was founded by deductions from the veterans' pay. This was followed by a system of facilities by the action of the Federal Government in 1865 and 1873.

Simultaneously, the various states were establishing their own facilities to treat the injuries and diseases of veterans regardless whether they were service-related. These provided care for those who served in the Civil War, Indian War, Spanish American War, Mexican border conflicts, the War of 1812, as well as members of the armed services who had not participated in any conflict.

World War I brought further advances in care for those who served. This included disability compensation and vocational rehabilitation. There were soon three separate federal agencies caring for veterans, and eligibility for services was expanded. It was President Hoover who consolidated the bureaus and programs into The Veterans Administration in 1930.

The scope of World War II severely limited the ability of the Veterans Administration to provide services to the Federal Board of Hospitalization which had been approved by President Franklin D. Roosevelt to provide care to those who had served. Soon there was not only insufficient medical personnel for the injured vets but also a lack of hospitals.

At the same time, there was an increase in the numbers of those requiring care for mental illness and tuberculosis, so that by the end of World War II, the VA was treating less than 10% of U.S. casualties.

There were two new programs implemented, however. The Disabled Veteran's Rehabilitation Act and the G.I. Bill. The purpose was to provide benefits and training. At the same time, the VA was swamped with the number of veterans whom they were to treat, the number expanding to more than eighteen million.

To deal with this, the number of hospitals was expanded by over a third to 130, the number of employees of the Administration to over 65,000 and the number of full-time doctors increased to 4,000. This resulted in an increase of the VA budget to half a billion dollars and the tripling of employment.

However, with all this, the Veterans Administration was unprepared to deal with what awaited them. The number of veterans looking to the VA for care and assistance after World War II was three times that after World War I. This is understandable because the Second War lasted more than twice as long, and the mobilization rate was three times greater. An example of this is the treatment of mental illness, including performing 2,000 lobotomies at VA hospitals. Additionally, electric shock therapy was regularly used even though the convulsions it caused were many times strong enough to break the patient's bones.

As each year went by, there were also increasing political turf wars, aging facilities, a 500% increase in patients, 171 hospitals, centralization in Washington, D.C., and numerous scandals. At the same time, there were increases in benefits and programs so that promised benefits included disability compensation, training, health care, loans, pensions, vocational rehabilitation, special social security benefits, and assisted living caregivers.

This combination was made all the more complex and eventually destructive by the growth of the bureaucracy and with the war's ending, resulting in budget cutbacks. The results were catastrophic. VA hospitals became "slums" with one nurse handling eighty patients at a time. Doctors described the conditions as "medieval" and "filthy." *Life Magazine*, May 1970.

Combat veteran and central character in *Born on the Fourth of July*, Ron Kovic, described laying in his own filth in his rat-infested hospital in New York City. Heroes waited days, weeks, months for treatment or even attention. Kovic interrupted Richard Nixon's nomination speech calling out, "…the leaders of this government threw me and others away to rot in their VA hospitals."

As noted above, the Veterans Administration has been the host of scandals many of which have affected our veterans. To best understand how reprehensible and heinous this is, one must understand that this was not an isolated incident or even a few events that affected some soldiers or only those from the Vietnam War. Rather it is a decades-old culture in which such scandals were repeated over and over.

Note, for instance, as described by CNN's Michael Pearson in "The VA's Troubled History": (a) that the Bureau established to provide benefits to those who served in World War I was abolished because of scandal; (b) federal troops had to use force to disrupt a demonstration by veterans for unpaid World War I bonuses; (c) The administrator of the VA under President Harry Truman resigned after reports of poor care in a number of facilities—enormous loss of funds to mismanagement was discovered the following year; (d) in 1976, the General Accounting Office found woeful patient care in the Denver and New Orleans VA hospitals; (e) in

1982, VA Director Nimmo resigned after referring to the results of exposure to Agent Orange as "teenage acne."

This went on and on during and after the Vietnam War, including negligent and reckless treatment at facilities in West Los Angeles, Chicago, North Carolina, Miami, Dayton, Pittsburgh, and Phoenix. There was also criminal activity, including falsification of records and the taking of bribes. There are findings of "systematic problems at health facilities nationwide." This extended into the Obama Administration long after President Reagan had elevated the Veterans Administration to a cabinet-level as the U.S. Department of Veterans Affairs.

And while it is hoped that The Veterans Affairs Accountability and Whistleblower Protection Act signed into law by President Trump in June of 2017 will put an end to the horrendous treatment of our veterans, is there reason to believe that it will? And what if it does? What will it do for those who have been victims for almost fifty years and will likely remain so until they join their deceased brothers, the Edison 64?

Dow Chemical and Monsanto were the two largest producers of the poisonous defoliant, Agent Orange. Along with many other chemical companies, they were responsible for the millions of cancers suffered by U.S. and Vietnamese soldiers, as well as generations of their children, due to the presence of the known carcinogen and poison, dioxin, which was present in the 20,000,000 gallons of lethal spray used with the knowledge of the effects by the United States military.

Now the VA recognizes numerous cancers, Parkinson's Disease, diabetes, birth defects and other horrors as caused by the defoliant. Does it matter now that those veterans may receive a check from the government after years and years of waiting? How much is that cancer worth? What is the price of that suffering and the humiliation of being ignored?

The same can be said for the U.S. Department of Veteran Affairs and its National Center for PTSD. There have been decades of avoidance, lack of prevention and misinformation. Now that the Edison veterans, and all their brothers and sisters who served, have suffered thousands of nightmares, years of depression, acting out, hiding, even suicide, as described in the preceding chapter, how should the behavior of the Veterans Administration be received? The answer is with guilt and shame.

Chapter Ten

Memorials

Monuments and memorials are for the living and the dead, reminders of great lives lived and lost. They are both in honor and memory of the Edison 64.

There is the solid bronze plaque in the main entrance to the school, which also has a memorial garden. The Commonwealth of Pennsylvania installed a historic marker through the Pennsylvania Historical & Museum Commission. A playground was named after Gerry Maguire and a street was named "Edison 64 Memorial Street." The names of the 64 are forever on the walls in Philadelphia and Washington. There is now the Lural Lee Blevins housing for Vietnam veterans.

Each Memorial Day the high school has a dramatic and uplifting assembly with Dr. Darryrl Johnson as the Master of Ceremonies. There are speeches, songs, guest speakers and a presentation of gifts including a thousand-dollar scholarship. The event culminates in the presentation of a wreath, a 21-gun salute, the playing of Taps and a balloon release.

To those in attendance who served in the Vietnam War, and the family members of those who lost their lives and their supporters, it is significant and dramatic. Yet, at the same time, it can never be enough.

Following are photos of these monuments.

Monuments and Memorials

The following photos are all courtesy of:
Mr. Patrick J. Hughes,
www.patrickjhughes.org

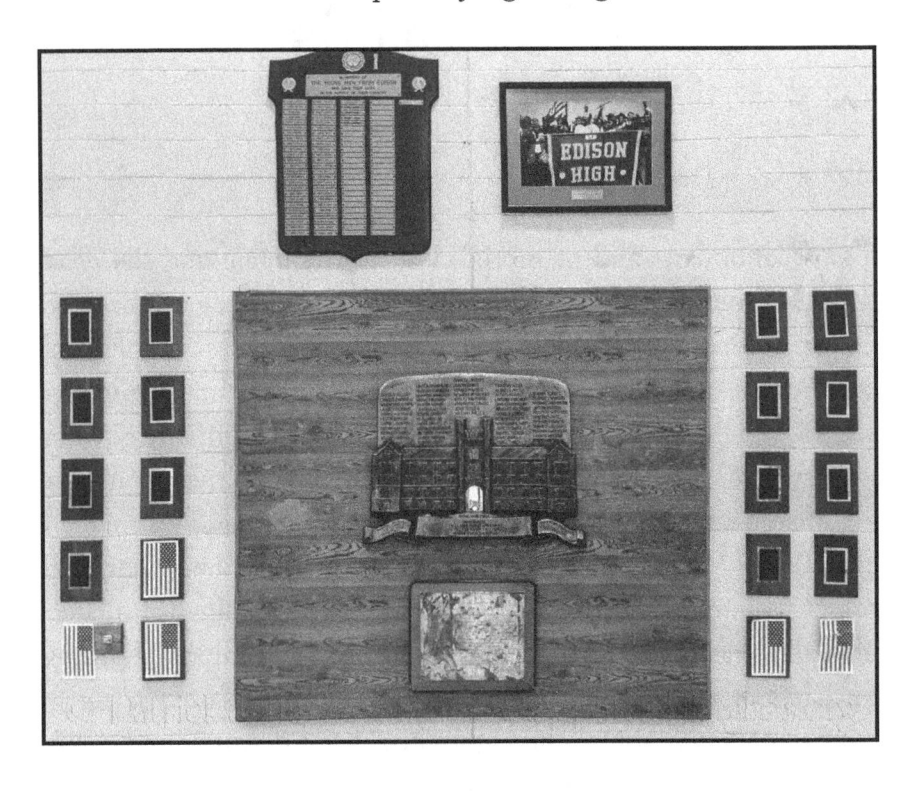

Memorials

215

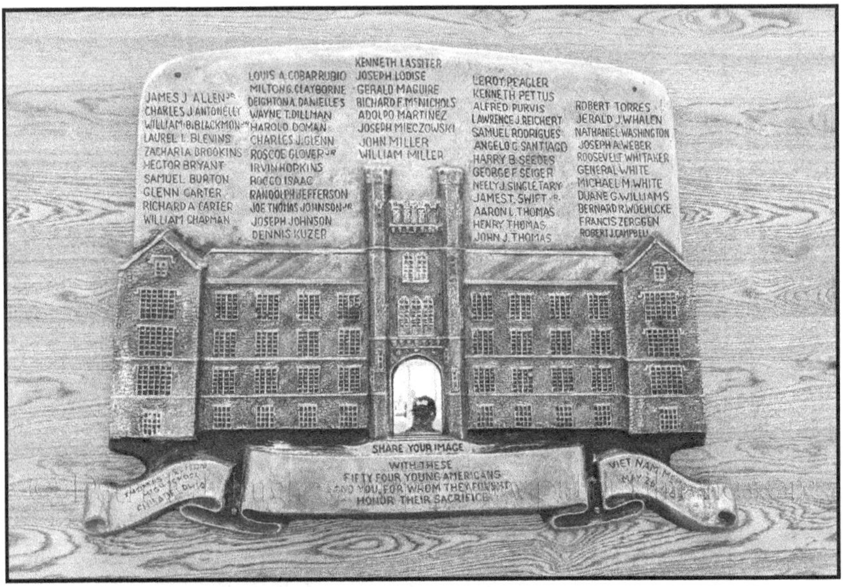
KENNETH LASSITER
LOUIS A. COBARRUBIO
JOSEPH LODISE
MILTON G. CLAYBORNE
GERALD MAGUIRE
LEROY PEAGLER
KENNETH PETTUS
JAMES J. ALLEN JR
CHARLES J. ANTONELLI
WILLIAM B. BLACKMON JR
LAUREL L. BLEVINS
ZACHARIA BROOKINS
HECTOR BRYANT
SAMUEL BURTON
GLENN CARTER
RICHARD A. CARTER
WILLIAM CHAPMAN
DEIGHTON A. DANIELLE'S
WAYNE T. DILLMAN
HAROLD DOMAN
CHARLES J. GLENN
ROSCOE GLOVER JR
IRVIN HOPKINS
ROCCO ISAAC
RANDOLPH JEFFERSON
JOE THOMAS JOHNSON JR
JOSEPH JOHNSON
DENNIS KUZER
RICHARD F. McNICHOLS
ADOLPO MARTINEZ
JOSEPH MIECZOWSKI
JOHN MILLER
WILLIAM MILLER
ALFRED PURVIS
LAWRENCE J. REICHERT
SAMUEL RODRIGUES
ANGELO G. SANTIAGO
HARRY B. SEEDES
GEORGE F. SEIGER
NEELY J. SINGLETARY
JAMES T. SWIFT JR
AARON L. THOMAS
HENRY THOMAS
JOHN J. THOMAS
ROBERT TORRES
JERALD J. WHALEN
NATHANIEL WASHINGTON
JOSEPH A. WEBER
ROOSEVELT WHITAKER
GENERAL WHITE
MICHAEL M. WHITE
DUANE G. WILLIAMS
BERNARD R. WOEHLCKE
FRANCIS ZERGGEN
ROBERT J. CAMPBELL
SHARE YOUR IMAGE
WITH THESE
FIFTY FOUR YOUNG AMERICANS
AND YOU, FOR WHOM THEY FOUGHT
HONOR THEIR SACRIFICE

Memorials 217

The following photo courtesy of:
Mr. D. Miller, Graphics Instructor,
Thomas A. Edison, John C.
Fareira Skill Center

Edison/Fareira High School

Our Fallen Heroes

Honoring Edison's Extraordinary Young Men Who Gave Their Lives in Vietnam

Memorial Day 2017

Friday, May 26th

Memorials 219

The following two photos courtesy of:
Mr. Terry A. Williamson,
President,
Philadelphia Vietnam Veterans Memorial Fund

Poem

COME HOME MY VIETNAM VETS

Author, Robert Reilly
1964 Graduate Father Judge High School
US Army 1968–1970
Vietnam 1969–1970

William, Leo, and Al.
Come Home, Come Home, Come Home.
Some Say You Are Not Home Yet.
Come Home, Come Home, Come Home.
Come Home My Vietnam Vets.

To 1 Corps (Pronounced Eye Core)
2 Corps
3 Corps
4 Corps
And Mac V
Come Home, Come Home, Come Home.
Come Home My Vietnam Vets.

To The Fly Boys.
The Ground Boys.
The Arty Boys.
The Brown Water Boys.
And The Boys On The Deep Blue Sea.
To The Dollys, The Mollys, and the Marys.
Who Have Served So Faithfully.

Come Home, Come, Come Home, Come Home.
Come Home My Vietnam Vets.

Come Home, Come Home, Come Home
Some Say You Are Not Home Yet.

Come Home Come Home, Come Home.

We Want To Hug You.
We Thank You.
We Love You.
We Salute You.

Epilogue

On March 29, 2012, President Obama declared that day to be "National Vietnam War Veterans Day" in memorialization of what he declared to be the 50th Anniversary of our involvement in Vietnam. In his proclamation, he pointed to the "profound tragedy" that our servicemen and women were shunned and neglected upon their return instead of honoring them for their sacrifices and "serving them as they served us." The continuing scandalous treatment by the Veterans Administration tragically belied his words.

That single day for the Vietnam veterans became an annual day of celebration and honor by the Act of Congress, entitled the Vietnam War Veterans Recognition Act of 2017, which was signed by President Trump. However, the politically driven schism in our Country appears to grow with increasing violence. This makes it unlikely that the two pieces of our society will come together to honor and comfort those that sacrificed and so suffered until this day. Rather, it seems that Vietnam Veterans Day will likely inflame the inexplicable animosities that are threatening to further divide our Country by the pressures of hate, intolerance, and ignorance. Somehow, the phenomena of signs in restaurant windows announcing, "No military," the carrying of the Viet Cong flag and the adoration of the beret-wearing Che Guevara are still with us.

It is true that the daily barrage of war news, the chorus of "Hell no, we won't go," and the horror of the My Lai Massacre has morphed into other and new anti-American sentiment by a growing segment of our society. In a strange way, many anti-American Americans are adopting the hatred that preceded them by decades.

Thus, it must be known through the land that our servicemen do not deserve to be damned as "baby killers," then or now. The disturbing and frightening picture of that naked nine-year-old Vietnamese girl fleeing the incoming napalm should not be the immortalized image of our alleged atrocity. In fact, the bombing attacks shown did not involve the U.S. at all but rather were conducted entirely by the South Vietnamese Air Force.

Similarly, a lingering schism among our collective perception perpetuates the untruths about the Vietnam War. Our military in Vietnam was not composed primarily of the disadvantaged but rather was more than three-quarters middle class. It was not manned predominantly by draftees, but rather almost eighty percent by volunteers. And those who gave their lives were not mostly African Americans, but almost 85% were white.

As we are facing an increasing threat to our American values and unity, I feel it only appropriate that we embrace the words of Abraham Lincoln who, in commenting about the Civil War, declared, "Let the people know the truth and 'the country' is safe."

I pray that the preceding recollection of sacrifice and heroism, patriotism, and suffering, will in some small part serve to bring us back together again for then and only then will our Edison 64 and their brothers receive the honor and comfort they deserve.

To further reach this goal a portion of the proceeds of the sale of copies of this book shall be donated to veterans' causes.

Author's Note

The foregoing relates the history and happenings of the Edison 64 and their classmates who served but survived to suffer. It must be noted, however, that the Philadelphia Vietnam Veterans Memorial at Penn's Landing enshrines the names of 648 Philadelphians who gave their lives in the Vietnam War.

This includes the names of 27 men from nearby Father Judge High School and a similar number from the now-closed Cardinal Dougherty High School. Each number is the largest number from any Catholic High School in "the country" as Edison's 64 is the largest from any school in the United States.

It should be noted that Corporal Michael Crescenz, who had graduated from Cardinal Dougherty, posthumously received the Congressional Medal of Honor from President Richard Nixon in a White House Ceremony on April 7, 1970. The Philadelphia Veterans Affair Medical Center now bears the name of Corporal Crescenz.

About The Author

Richard Sand is a historian and award-winning author of a dozen books including *Girard College–A Living History*, *The Complete Handbook of Diplomatic, Official and Social Usage*, *The Lucas Rook Mystery Series* and *Tunnel Runner*, the acclaimed novel about the Vietnam War and its effects on those who experienced it.

Sand is also a practicing attorney and college professor, who served two governors as a member of the Pennsylvania Historical and Museum Commission. Mr. Sand was honored by the Pennsylvania State Senate for his contribution to the arts and is a member of the Pennsylvania Sports Hall of Fame. He is the founder of the Haym Solomon Society and a recipient of The Ben Franklin Award.

Mr. Sand is married to acclaimed educator and athlete, Kathie Daley. They have four children and three grandchildren.

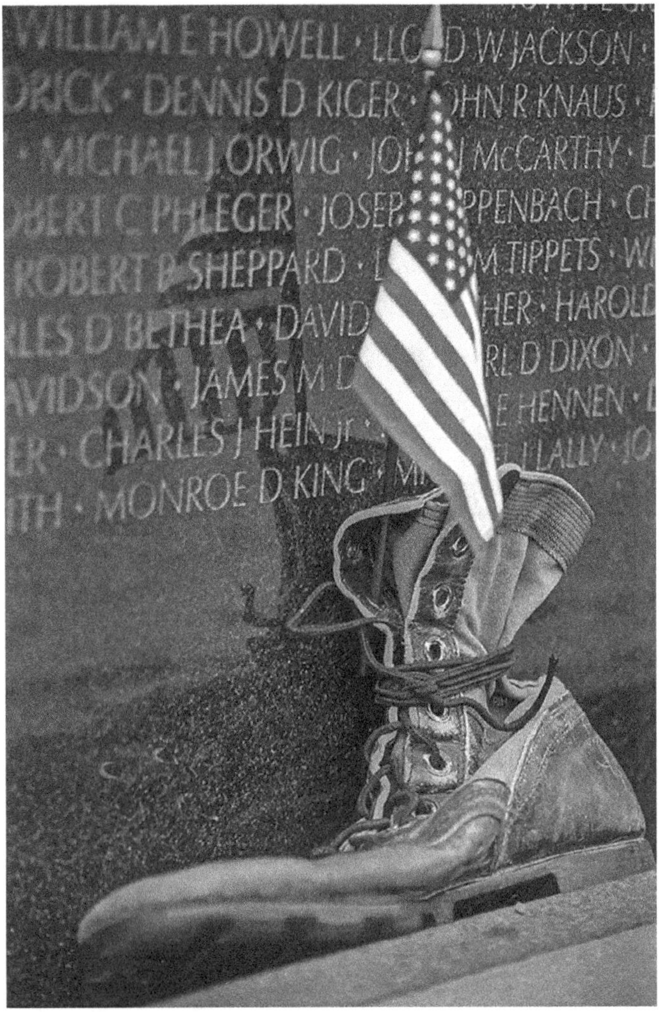